LK. 8/14
9/2016

THE FAMILY OF JESUS

 This Large Print Book carries the
Seal of Approval of N.A.V.H.

THE FAMILY OF JESUS

KAREN KINGSBURY

CHRISTIAN LARGE PRINT
A part of Gale, Cengage Learning

GALE
CENGAGE Learning®

Farmington Hills, Mich • San Francisco • New York • Waterville, Maine
Meriden, Conn • Mason, Ohio • Chicago

LIBRARY OF CONGRESS CATALOGING-IN-PUBLICATION DATA

Kingsbury, Karen.
    The family of Jesus / by Karen Kingsbury. — Large Print edition.
        pages cm. — (Christian Large Print originals)
    ISBN 978-1-4104-7044-7 (hardcover) — ISBN 1-4104-7044-X (hardcover)
    1. Jesus Christ—Family. 2. Bible—Biography. 3. Large type books. I. Title.
BT313.K56 2014b
232.9—dc23   2014016255

Published in 2014 by arrangement with Howard Books, a division of Simon & Schuster, Inc.

Printed in Mexico
1 2 3 4 5 6 7 18 17 16 15 14

Dear Reader Friends,

A long time ago I fell in love with the Bible. The truths and promises, the wisdom and complexities. And maybe most especially the people. When I read about those who made up the world Jesus walked in, I see them as they are described in the pages of the Bible. But I see so much more.

And so I began to ask God: What if I could write a series of short novels about these people? What if I could make up the details that aren't there and give readers a way to see these men and women as very real people with real pain and real problems?

The idea took root. The first people I felt compelled to write about were the family members of Jesus. Those closest to Him. The ones who celebrated His birth and protected Him, walked alongside Him, and sometimes felt most confused by Him. There was a cost to being in the family of Jesus back then.

Just as there is a cost to being in the family of Jesus today.

From the beginning as I undertook this project, I felt compelled by my love of the Bible to stick to some hard-and-fast ground rules. The most important was this: The stories had to be anchored in Scripture. In

5

a way, I took the Bible verses on these real-life characters and stuck them like tent stakes in the desert sand. Nothing could ever violate those truths.

Then I researched the cultural and geographical accuracy and made absolutely sure the tent of the stories didn't billow beyond that.

But otherwise, I let the tent blow in the wind a little.

Did Joseph bring Mary wild orchids? Did Elizabeth and Zechariah live long enough to see John the Baptist beheaded? Was James watching the crucifixion of Christ from a distance, still embarrassed by His claim that He was God?

We cannot possibly know from what we've been given in Scripture.

And so I asked myself this question, and I asked those with theological training the same question: Is it possible? Given the anchors of Scripture and the boundaries of culture and geography, are these things possible? When the answer was yes — I told a story.

I remember hearing from my wonderful editor, Becky Nesbitt, when she finished reading this book for the first time. "Wow," she told me. "I have tears streaming down my face, and I've never loved Jesus more.

People are going to go crazy over this."

That, then, has remained my prayer.

You see, sometimes life can leave a layer of complacency over the things we love. Even something as precious as the Bible. Of course, the Bible is never complacent. It is the Living Word, alive and active and useful for teaching, affirming, correcting, and training in righteousness. The two things that will live forever are the word of God and the souls of mankind.

But even so, I believe these stories on the family of Jesus will make you fall more in love with God's word than ever before. I believe they will give you a front-row seat and make you more compassionate toward the people who walked closest with Jesus: Joseph and Mary, Jesus's earthly parents. John the Baptist, the cousin of Jesus. Zechariah and Elizabeth, considered by theologians and cultural time-period experts to be the aunt and uncle of Jesus. And James, the brother of Jesus.

Finally, please be assured that my pastor, Jamie George, helped me with the Bible study section you are about to read. I am not a biblical scholar. I am a student of the Bible. I love it, and I hold unswervingly to its infallibility. My storytelling is simply that — one way of looking at the stories of these people based on what I found in the Bible, what I know of the culture, and what the time would've allowed. I asked Jamie if what I wrote was possible. He used his theology degree and years of research to respond. When he didn't believe it was possible, I changed the story to something that could have been.

So sit back and let the sights and sounds and wonder of the family of Jesus fill your heart. Thanks for taking this journey with me, and please visit my website at KarenKingsbury.com to sign up for my newsletter and hear more about future books and Bible studies.

See you at the back of the book!

In His light and love,
Karen Kingsbury

Dedicated to . . .

Donald, who has always believed I should do my part to help bring the Bible to life. You were the one who first shared Scripture with me: "Hey, before that movie, would it be okay if we read the Bible together?" You're the most wonderful man of God, my love. I wouldn't be a Christian, a writer, or in the most amazing family without you. How could the girl who once threw your Bible and broke the binding be writing a Bible study? Thanks for putting up with me all those years ago. God is faithful beyond words. I love you, Donald.

And to Kelsey, Kyle, Tyler, Sean, Josh, EJ, and Austin. May you always know the passion your father and I have for God's word, and may you live your lives anchored and rooted in Scripture, passionate for our Lord always. I love you all with all I am.

And to God Almighty, who has — for now — blessed me with these.

CONTENTS

11

STORY 1
JOSEPH
THE PROTECTIVE STEPFATHER

The wild orchids distracted him.

Joseph had been busy that day. He and his dad worked on a new house being built at the edge of town, and then this afternoon Joseph finished a food cart and two chairs. Now he was working on the gift no one knew about.

The little prayer table.

For months Joseph had been gathering beautiful cuts of olive wood, and when the day's tasks were done he would cut the pieces into sections and polish them until the grain shone like glass. The table was assembled now, the joints fastened. Joseph studied his work and smiled.

Once they were married, he and Mary would come together at this table in the early morning before the Lord, reflecting on God's Word and lifting their requests and praises before Him. Four hundred years of silence hung over the Jewish people since the last prophet had spoken on behalf of God. Now all of Israel was waiting. For a sign or a prophet.

For the Messiah.

Joseph imagined sitting at the prayer table with Mary, joining their people by praying for answers, praying for deliverance. He dreamed about the time, a year from now, when he could share that life with her. Joseph tenderly moved the small table to the corner of his workshop. Other nights he might've worked later, but this was Wednesday — the one day each week when he visited Mary. Today would be even more special because of the orchids.

He put away his tools, swept the earthen floor, and then — with the sun just beginning to set — he hurried out to the field behind the carpenter shop. For a moment he studied the spray of purple orchids and he felt a smile take over his face. Mary loved orchids. One day soon he would build her a home with a view of this very field.

So that Mary could have orchids as often as spring allowed.

"Orchids are God's reminder that we can always start over," she would tell him. He brought them to her as often as he could.

Joseph gathered a full bouquet and then stopped at the doorway of his parents' house. "Going to Mary's." He smiled at his mother.

"Give her our love." His mother nodded at him. "And her parents also."

"I will." Joseph was anxious. He looked forward all week to this day. "Be back in a few hours."

"Son." His mother stood, and her eyes looked deeper than before. Slowly she came to him.

"Yes."

"I'm proud of you, if I haven't said so in a while. Your work . . . your faith . . . the way you love Mary." She nodded, more emotional, as if she was trying to find the right words. "You're a righteous young man, Joseph. I'm a blessed woman indeed."

Joseph lowered the bouquet of orchids. "Thank you. That means a lot."

"I don't say it enough." His mother reached out and hugged him, the sort of hug that could say more than a thousand words. She stepped back. "Now go see that beautiful girl of yours."

Joseph thought about his mother's words all the way to Mary's house. Did she really see him that way — righteous? He was only twenty years old, with nowhere near enough experience to be wise or mature. Still, his parents thought he was a good man. It was the greatest compliment anyone could've given him, and Joseph knew he'd remember his mother's words always.

The street was busy, with men and women gathered in the fronts of various houses sharing the day's business or the condition of crops in the distant fields. In Joseph's mind, Nazareth shone brighter than other towns in Israel. The people were closer-knit, friendlier. Children grew up and stayed in Nazareth, sharing in each other's lives for decades. Joseph knew all his neighbors' first names, their trials and triumphs, the depth of their faith. Almost as if the entire town were one big family. Nazareth was home. Joseph had loved growing up here, and in the years to come this was where he and Mary would raise their family.

Joseph could hardly wait.

He rounded a corner and saw her house, on a modest lot of land near the edge of town. Often this time of night Mary would be out back, staring at the distant valley, praying to God or dreaming of the days ahead. Joseph walked in that direction and sure enough: she was sitting on a blanket, her long dark hair blowing in the breeze. He walked without a sound, but she must have sensed he was near because she turned to him. "Joseph!"

He stopped, his feet frozen in place, the flowers at his side. For a long moment, he simply admired her. Her honey-smooth complexion and the fine features of her profile. The way her eyes caught the light from the setting sun. She hurried to her feet and ran to him. Joseph caught her in his arms.

He ran his hand along the back of her head and then carefully distanced himself from her. "I've missed you."

"Me, too." She looked breathless, her face all lit up. "Seeing you . . . it's the best part of the week."

He wished he could hug her again, hold her longer than a few seconds. But that would have to wait. Joseph held up the orchids. "For you."

Her eyes softened. She took the flowers and breathed in their fragrance. "You always do that."

"Do what?" He maintained the space between them. He could visit Mary once a week and greet her with a hug. Even hold hands now and then. But nothing more.

"Nice things." Mary stared at the flowers and then lifted her eyes to him. "For no reason."

Joseph felt his smile fade. "You're my reason, Mary. Now and always."

"Orchids are my favorite." She smiled at him. "I just wish . . ." She looked to the valley beyond.

"What do you wish?" He started walking back to her blanket in the grass. She fell in step beside him.

Mary waited until they sat down before she caught his gaze again. "I wish we were getting married tomorrow. A year seems so long."

"Hmmm. For me, too." He watched her set the flowers at the corner of the blanket and lean back on her hands.

Her smile melted his heart. "If only I weren't so young."

She had a point. Custom required couples to wait a year after they were betrothed. And Joseph and Mary had been betrothed only a short while. "It's our parents' fault." He chuckled, teasing her. "They should've arranged this a long time ago."

"I know." Mary's sweet laughter joined his. "What were they thinking?"

Joseph took Mary's hand and worked his fingers through hers. They had known each other forever, as far back as either of them could remember. A little silence between them was comfortable.

18

Moments like this, Joseph couldn't help but go back to the beginning. When he was little more than a boy, Joseph's family had spent time with Mary's family during one long holiday. As the night fell, Joseph found Mary with the other kids near the river. He pulled her aside and took her hand. "I'm going to marry you when we grow up," he told her.

She had blushed and giggled. "That's not your choice."

"Doesn't matter." He remembered sticking his chest out. "It'll happen. I just think so."

In fact, lots of men Joseph's age would've chosen Mary. But the friendship between Joseph and Mary's families worked in Joseph's favor and it became the answer to his prayers. It was really going to happen. He was going to marry the girl of his dreams.

"What are you thinking?" Mary's voice was soft, like music on the wind.

Joseph grinned. "How great God is, letting me have you for the rest of my life."

She looked down at her lap, her smile lifting her pretty mouth. When she caught his gaze, her innocence shone brighter than the setting sun. "God is so great, Joseph." She looked at the valley again. "I love talking to Him. Seeking His will." She found Joseph's eyes. "I've done that since I was a little girl."

Joseph took a deep breath and admired Mary. Everyone knew about her faith. More than any of the young women in town, Mary loved God, and the proof showed in her eyes. He ran his thumb along Mary's hand and breathed in deep, enjoying the clear spring air. "I feel God has something big for us, Mary. Right here in Nazareth."

"Like what?" She angled her head, admiration bright in her expression. "A bigger carpentry shop?"

"Maybe." Joseph narrowed his eyes and watched the streaky sky. "I don't know. I just feel it." It was getting late, so he helped her to her feet. "Whatever God has ahead, as long as I'm with you, I'm ready."

Mary didn't say anything. The look in her eyes told him she agreed with every word, and whatever God had planned for them, they were ready.

They would face it together.

Joseph wasn't sure when the trouble began. Had he said something that offended Mary or scared her? Either way, she was gone to Jerusalem, to her cousin Elizabeth's house in the hill country of Judea. She had left just one very clear instruction.

Tell Joseph not to follow me.

That was three months ago. Three long, unbearable months.

It was late afternoon, the day's work done, and Joseph paced the carpenter shop, kicking up dirt from the floor. Every time he passed the window he stopped and stared out. The orchids had faded in the scorching summer heat and now only a few of the purple flowers dotted the fields and valleys around Nazareth.

Joseph looked at the prayer table. It was finished now. Ready for the future. The only reminder of that awful Wednesday when he'd walked to her house and found her gone. Her mother had cried when she gave him the news. Mary wasn't home. She'd joined a caravan from Nazareth and headed to her cousin's house, not far from Jerusalem.

"She gave no explanation." Her mother had clearly been confused. "Of course I trust her. Mary has never given me a reason to doubt." She paused. "But I have no answers. I'm so sorry, Joseph."

The earth might as well have opened up and swallowed Joseph whole. Jerusalem was a five-day walk from Nazareth. Mary had been fine the week before. Why in the world would she leave? And why hadn't she wanted him to follow her? Why hadn't she told him?

Joseph had been worried sick over her absence every day since. Not only that, but after so much time, people in Nazareth were beginning to talk. Like him, they wondered why Mary would go to Jerusalem, alone. Why hadn't she told Joseph about her plans, and what had she been doing these past three months?

He paced again and stopped at the open door. *Dear God, where is she? I love her more than my own life.* He waited, listening. A summer storm approached on the horizon, but he heard no voice of God, no assurance that Mary still loved him or wanted to marry him.

No certainty that she was even alive.

Father, please . . . protect my Mary. Keep her safe as she's so far from home. Please, God. Joseph didn't care about the talk around town. Sure, he took a few questionable glances and yes, people whispered more when he walked down the street. Never mind any of that. All he cared about was Mary. Knowing that she'd arrived safely at her cousin's house . . . holding out hope that she'd come home soon.

He walked slowly back to the corner of the shop and ran his hand over the prayer table.

His fingers traced the swirly grain of the wood, the glossiness of the surface. He was about to pray once more for Mary's safe return when he heard someone yelling. Joseph thought he recognized the voice. He ran to the door and saw a young boy running toward him, his sandals slapping hard at the road beneath his feet. Joseph knew him immediately. He was the youngest son of the family who lived next door to Mary.

Joseph hurried to meet the child. "What is it? What happened?" he called out, his tone desperate.

"Mary!" The boy's grin stretched across his face. "She's back! She just came home! My mama told me to come tell you!"

And just like that, Joseph felt his world right itself.

Mary was alive and she was back. He would go to her and they would talk and she would explain everything: why she left and the reason she was gone so long and how come she didn't want him to follow her. In a few hours it would all make sense.

As soon as he could talk to Mary.

Joseph didn't quit running until he reached her house, but the moment he saw her he stopped cold. Mary was sitting on her favorite blanket behind the house, facing the distant fields and valleys. Even from here he wanted only to take in the sight of her, his heart pounding out his relief, his legs trembling. He had missed her every day, every hour.

Now, finally, she was home. She was here. And she was his.

Before he could hurry the rest of the way to her side, he caught a glimpse of her profile and in the time it took to breathe in, something happened. Doubt rained over the moment. She was changed. Her expression or her posture. As if she'd aged a decade in three months. A shiver of fear ran down his neck.

Whatever had happened since the last time he saw her, Joseph had the feeling the news was going to change their lives. The closer he came to her, the more sure he was about the change. Her eyes were different. Guarded, or maybe deep with resolve.

"Mary . . ." He held out his hand but she didn't take it.

"Sit with me. Please." She slid over and nodded to the empty spot on the blanket. "I have something to tell you."

Joseph's heart beat so hard he could barely breathe. He sat down and searched her eyes, her face. "I missed you."

Her expression softened. "I missed you,

too." Mary drew a slow, deep breath, never breaking eye contact. "Joseph . . . I'm pregnant."

The world stopped spinning.

Joseph could feel himself falling . . . falling someplace dark and deep and otherworldly. What had she said? Mary was pregnant? No, that couldn't be it. But those were her words, and now . . . He managed to stand and walk to the edge of the bluff. *Breathe, Joseph. You have to breathe.* She couldn't be pregnant unless . . .

Shock flooded his veins, rushed at his heart, but already another emotion was rising to the surface. A sort of pain Joseph had never known before. He hung his head. What was he supposed to do next? How could he —

"Joseph." She had followed him, her tone urgent. She took gentle hold of his shoulder. "There's more. Please . . ."

He took a step closer to the edge of the bluff, away from her touch. There was more? He turned to her. If only she didn't look so beautiful. Even now, when she was breaking his heart. "What?" He shrugged. "What else is there?"

"It's not what you think." Mary had never looked so upset and so at peace, all at the same time. "I was . . . visited by an angel."

25

He stared at her and no words came. None at all. He had to be dreaming because nothing made sense. "An angel, Mary? Really?"

"Yes." She paused. "Joseph, you have to believe me." A calm came over her. She stood a little straighter, her expression set. "I haven't been with a man. I love only you."

The hurt was so great he had to remind himself to exhale. "You were gone three months."

"I left after . . . after the angel talked to me."

Joseph was too dazed to do anything but stand and listen. Maybe if he gave her a chance to tell her story a clap of thunder would sound and he would wake up. He folded his arms and braced himself.

The breeze caught Mary's hair and she squinted, her eyes locked on his. "It was the night after you brought me orchids. I was out back, behind my house down the valley." She caught her hair with one hand and held it. "I know you tell me not to go too far away from the house alone, but the stars were beautiful and I needed to pray. Down in the valley, that's my favorite place. Just God and me."

Her story picked up speed now that he was letting her talk. "I sat on the big rock,

26

and just as I started to talk to the Lord, this . . . this angel man appeared."

Joseph shook his head and stared at the ground. When he looked up he saw tears in Mary's eyes. The first time he'd ever seen her cry. He tried to keep his hurt and anger in check. "What did this . . . angel say?"

She dabbed at her eyes, her voice steady despite her obvious sadness. "I'm not making this up, Joseph. You have to believe me."

"I'm trying."

"Okay." Mary sniffed and breathed in. "He told me the craziest thing I've ever heard. He greeted me and told me he was the angel Gabriel. Then he told me I was highly favored. He said the Lord was with me." She looked back at the blanket. "Please . . . can we sit down? I'm tired."

Joseph fought off his hurt. He followed her to the blanket and as they sat, he faced her, leaving more space than usual. "Go on."

"I was scared to death, of course. I mean, he was real, Joseph. Like a man only all dressed in white and he, I don't know, he . . . sort of glowed." Mary shook her head and stared at the valley beyond. "I thought I would pass out or my heart would stop." She looked at Joseph. "But he told me not to be afraid. Then he said it again — that I'd found favor with God."

One thing was certain. Mary believed the story. Joseph could see that much in her eyes.

"What he said next . . ." Her voice fell, and she looked nervous for the first time. She seemed to gather her strength. "He told me I was going to conceive and give birth to a son. I'm supposed to call Him Jesus."

"Jesus." Joseph blinked.

"Yes. Jesus." She put her hand on her stomach, protective. "The boy — my baby — the angel said He would grow to be great, and that . . . He would be called the Son of the Most High." Her tone filled with awe. "Son of the Most High, Joseph. The child inside me." She hesitated. "The angel said God would give this boy the throne of His father, David . . . and that He would reign over Jacob's descendants forever." Her voice dropped to barely a whisper, her eyes wide. "He told me Jesus's kingdom would never end."

Again Joseph wanted to run or shout or find some way out of this insane conversation. Mary had never acted like this, never talked this way. Whatever had happened over the last three months, he couldn't begin to make sense of it.

"I know . . . I didn't understand, either." She folded her hands in her lap and lifted her eyes to the sky. "I asked the angel how any of this could be. I told him I'm . . . I'm a virgin."

Joseph clenched his jaw, struggling.

"But he said the Holy Spirit would come over me and . . . the power of the Most High would overshadow me." Her breathing picked up some. "This is the hardest part. He said . . . this baby boy would be the Son of God. Those were his exact words."

That was all Joseph could take.

He stood and stared at Mary for a few heartbeats. Then he turned and walked to the edge of the bluff once more. The Son of God? Only one deserved that title: the Messiah. The Savior. The one the Hebrew people had waited hundreds of years to see.

Was she serious? Mary wanted him to believe the baby in her womb was the Son of God? He felt sick. Shocked, and hurt, and angry. He needed to get away from here, away from her. When he turned around she was there, standing a few feet away, pain and heartache written across her face. He shook his head. "I need to go."

"I'm telling the truth." Tears filled her eyes again. "After that, the angel told me . . . about Elizabeth. My cousin. The angel said she was going to have a child, too. And that she was six months along."

He controlled his emotions. "Your cousin?"

"Yes. The last thing he said was that no word from God would ever fail."

Joseph felt a ripple of fear. "You know what you're saying, right? You're talking about the Messiah. That's not something to make up."

"I . . . am . . . not making this up." For the first time Mary sounded upset. Almost angry.

"Okay." From the depths of his heart Joseph felt the slightest compassion begin to stir. If he wasn't dreaming, whatever had happened with Mary, she believed it. Absolutely. Maybe she'd lost her mind, but she believed the crazy story. Even if it bordered on blasphemous. "That's why you went to Judea? Because the . . . angel told you Elizabeth was pregnant?"

"Yes! Exactly!" She stood straighter, hopeful. "I mean, I told the angel that I was the Lord's servant. I said, 'May your word to me be fulfilled.' " She blinked, clearly overwhelmed by the experience. "Then he left. He was gone as quickly as he appeared." She stared at Joseph, right through him. "I had to go to Elizabeth. First, before I talked to anyone else. Because if it was true about her being six months' pregnant, then . . . well, then everything the angel said had to be true."

"And?" Joseph's tone was more in control, but the shock hadn't let up.

Mary took her time, as if her next words were sacred. "It was just as the angel said. Elizabeth was pregnant and . . . when I walked in she said her baby leapt in her womb." Again she put her hand over her flat stomach. "She already knew . . . She called me the mother of her Lord. Really, Joseph. I'm serious."

He'd heard all he could take. But for all the heartache and disbelief flooding his heart, he knew this — he couldn't be angry with Mary. She was pregnant and she believed her strange, unreal story. Both things would forever change the plans they'd had three months ago. Joseph steadied himself. No matter what had happened he loved her too much to be angry, too much to use harsh words or disdain.

Joseph took a step back. "I need to leave."

"But . . ." Fresh hurt darkened her eyes. "I want to tell you about Elizabeth and John, about my time there."

"Later." He closed the distance between them and touched her shoulder for a brief moment. He still loved her so much. "I have to get back." He felt the sadness in his expression. If she'd committed adultery, the penalty was too great to consider. He exhaled, defeated. "I have a lot to think about, Mary. About us . . . about what happens next."

She hung her head, broken, and for a few seconds he wondered if she might admit the truth about the pregnancy. Something more believable than an angel and the Son of God. Instead she lifted her eyes one last time. "Go." A new strength seemed to resonate from her soul. "I will pray that God shows you the truth."

Joseph nodded. And with a final look, he turned and walked home from Mary's house, down the main street and past the fields of fading orchids. The whole time he was consumed with just one thought.

His betrothal to Mary was finished.

Joseph couldn't eat or sleep. His parents asked him about Mary, but he could only shake his head. "I need a few hours. I'll talk then."

He went out back and took the trail behind his house to the valley floor. Maybe here he could somehow gain understanding. Joseph found a smooth ledge, sat down, and stared straight ahead. If an angel were going to visit him, this would be a great time. But he heard only the summer breeze and utter silence.

The facts stood like armed soldiers, swords drawn and aimed straight at his heart. Mary was pregnant. After being gone three months without warning she was home and she was going to have a baby. Rather than come out and say what happened, whom she'd been with, or how the guy had wormed his way into her life, she'd come up with a story no one would believe. What was he supposed to do? Stay with her? What would their friends and family think? His reputation would be destroyed right alongside hers. And if Mary tried to use the angel story to explain herself, things would get worse.

He and Mary would be unrighteous *and* crazy.

Why had she turned her back on him and their dreams? How could she have been with another man when she had always loved him? Only him. The valley walls felt as if they were closing in around him. If he called her out, if he reported her, then she would face a certain ending.

She would be taken to the city limits and stoned.

The love of his life. His Mary.

He wasn't dreaming. Mary was pregnant

and despite her nonsensical ramblings, one thing was true: he wasn't the father. She had to be out of her mind, because the Mary he knew would never have betrayed him. Never. Joseph put his hands over his face and for the first time since he'd heard the news, he let the tears come.

Angry, desperate, heartbroken tears. No matter what Mary had done, regardless of the reason, he still loved her. He couldn't bear to see her stoned to death. They might as well stone him, too. The sobs shook his shoulders and made it hard to breathe. What was he supposed to do? He wiped his face with the back of his hands and stood, looking one direction and then the next. As if there might be some way out. But there was none.

None except one.

Joseph lifted his eyes to the hills, his jaw clenched. "Where does my help come from?" The broken cry filled the air. He pushed on, determined. "My help comes from the Lord." He gritted his teeth even as hot tears made their way down his cheek. "The Maker of heaven and earth."

Yes, the psalmist was right. Joseph had known the words to the Holy Scriptures since he was a boy. They had never meant more. "Help me, God . . . You neither slumber nor sleep. Help me now."

The breeze kicked up a spray of loose dirt and it turned to mud on Joseph's tear-stained face. He wiped it with his shirt, clearing his eyes. When he could see again he raised both hands to heaven. "Why, God?" His sides heaved. "Help me!"

The sun was setting, and Joseph knew better than to be here alone after dark. Leopards and hyenas would smell him and sense his vulnerability. He looked across the valley floor and to the sky once more. No angels here. A numbness came over him and gradually his eyes dried. He climbed the hill. He couldn't really feel his feet.

With every step the reality hit him again.

Back at the house he found his father. Joseph must've looked awful, because his dad stood slowly and came to him. "Son, what is it?"

The story took most of an hour to sort through. Joseph's father was quiet, the weight of the situation heavy around them. After a long time, Joseph clenched his fists. "They can't kill her." His head hurt and he ached from the hole where his heart used to be. "I can't let them do it."

Sadness replaced the shock in his father's eyes. Slowly he nodded and took a deep breath. "Do you have any ideas? What to do next?"

Joseph was desperate for a way out. Suddenly an idea came to him. "I suppose I could . . . I could file a divorce decree quietly, without bringing attention to it . . . And maybe the religious leaders would think the two of us separated before this . . . before she . . ."

"I understand." The older man seemed to know that Joseph couldn't finish the sentence.

The pain of Mary's unfaithfulness would remain until his last breath. But Mary's life might be spared if the idea worked. Joseph nodded. "It's a good plan. I'll try it."

Joseph had never felt more exhausted. He dragged himself to bed, but before he fell asleep he pictured her again. Mary. The only girl he'd ever loved. He rolled on his side and stared into the darkness. *I trust You, God. But I never imagined this.* He closed his eyes. Tomorrow he would file the divorce decree. He would do everything in his power to keep it quiet. He closed his eyes. What he really needed was a miracle, that tomorrow morning he would wake up and all of this would be nothing more than a bad dream. Mary would be pure. She would be home.

And she would be his.

Joseph was in the deepest sleep he'd had in ages when a light fell around him. He was still sleeping. He knew that. But the light grew brighter, more brilliant than anything Joseph had ever seen or imagined. Terror gripped him and the overpowering light blinded him. Before he could move or speak, a voice called out, "Joseph, do not be afraid."

Joseph's heart slammed against his chest and he shielded his eyes, barely squinting into the light. "Who . . . who are you?"

"I am the angel of the Lord." The voice was strong and sure, full of peace.

Terror seized him. What was this? His body began to shake and gradually his eyes adjusted. He could see the angel standing beside his bed. He sat up a little straighter, his teeth chattering. He could barely focus above the sound of his pounding heart. "What . . . do you want from me?"

"Joseph, son of David, do not be afraid to take Mary home as your wife, because what is conceived in her is from the Holy Spirit."

The Holy Spirit? Joseph felt the hair on his neck stand up. That's what Mary had said. Her words exactly. The baby in her was from God alone. He blinked a few times and nodded. "Mary told me that."

A look of utter truth shone in the angel's face. "She will give birth to a son, and you are to give Him the name Jesus, because He will save His people from their sins."

Before Joseph could speak, the angel was gone and it was morning. Joseph woke up and climbed out of bed, breathing hard, his heart pounding. Whatever had happened during his sleep, he knew one thing: God had sent the angel as an answer to his prayers.

Now he had to find Mary.

Never mind that the sun was barely up, Joseph dressed quickly and hurried through town to get to her. He reached her house and again found her outside, staring at the distant valley, sitting on the same blanket as the night before. She probably hadn't slept. She must've been deeply hurt by Joseph's reaction, afraid of all she might face if he didn't believe her.

She stood as he walked up and this time Joseph didn't hesitate. He hugged her, a desperate sort of hug. "The angel," he told her as he drew back, "he visited me, too. Everything you said, it was true."

Mary hesitated, as if she needed time for his words to reach the depths of her heart.

"Really?" Joy dawned gradually in her eyes and her smile spoke of how desperately she needed him. "I told you."

"Our family . . . our friends." He searched her eyes. "They'll never believe us."

"No. But we have each other." Sadness colored her expression, even as her smile remained. "And one day generations will believe."

Generations. Joseph felt the weight of the responsibility. His voice fell to a whisper. "You're carrying the Savior of the world, Mary. The Messiah. The One our people have been waiting for."

"It's all I can think about."

He took hold of her hands. "None of this will be easy. You know that."

She nodded, her eyes lost in his. "I have you."

"Yes. Always." Love and loyalty and a fierce protection welled up in Joseph. "I will stay by your side every step of the way. Whatever happens, I will be here, Mary. Nothing will harm you and the baby, not as long as I am living." He looked deep into her eyes. "You will never be alone."

"Never." Tears filled her eyes. "We'll get through this together."

The whispers around town started when

Mary was in her seventh month.

At least their parents believed them — reluctantly, but still, Mary and Joseph had their support. The same wasn't true for the rest of Nazareth. At first it was just a murmur from a few shopkeepers as Mary walked by, but quickly the news spread through all of Nazareth. Joseph hated the way even the young girls whispered and pointed at Mary. He went to her early one morning. Again they met in the field behind her house. Joseph took her hands. "I can't stand this. We have to do something."

From the first day Mary returned from Judea she'd had a supernatural peace about her. But in that moment she looked scared to death. "What if they . . . stone me?"

"I talked to my father about that. If I don't press charges, then no one will think you've been with another man."

"But they think you and I . . ."

The breeze off the canyon played around them for a few minutes. Neither of them spoke. Finally Joseph drew a deep breath and straightened his shoulders. "I don't care what they think about me. It's you, Mary." He took her in his arms and ran his hand along her back. "You don't deserve this."

Her cheeks were wet when they drew back. "God chose me to carry the Savior."

She dabbed at her tears. "No other girl can say that."

Joseph looked at her, and then with the gentlest touch he placed his hand alongside her face. "You're so brave, Mary. I love you more than ever before." He paused. "I think it's time you stay inside more. With your parents. Until the baby comes."

The fear in her face eased, but a desperate concern remained. "Will you . . . come to see me still?"

"As often as I can . . . without harming your reputation." He allowed himself to be lost in her innocent eyes. "God will help us survive."

The hours passed slowly, painfully. When Joseph couldn't stand the whispers and gossip, he went to the religious leaders and told them the truth. The whole truth. Clearly the men were shocked, stroking their beards and nodding in disbelief. They didn't call Joseph a liar, but they asked a hundred questions until Joseph had repeated himself too many times to count.

In the end the meeting didn't help at all. The conversation with the religious leaders never became fact on the streets of Nazareth. If people got wind of the story, it only fanned the flames of gossip. Not only was

Mary pregnant out of wedlock, but she and Joseph had cooked up some insane idea about the baby being the Messiah. Joseph could practically hear the townspeople as he passed them on the way to Mary's house.

The pain and humiliation continued until a distraction came along.

It came in the form of a decree passed randomly and without notice by Emperor Augustus. The decree called for a census of all of Israel, which meant every man was to report to the city of his birth to be counted. For Joseph, that meant a weeklong trip by donkey to Bethlehem. Of course there was one problem.

Mary was days away from delivering.

The contractions had been coming off and on for two days. Joseph liked to think he could care for Mary and protect her on a journey like the one to Bethlehem. Instead, problems began their first day out. The nights were colder than he anticipated, and their food supply was questionable. Mary felt sick most of the time and their pace was only about half what it should be — especially with the baby almost here.

Joseph kept his eyes straight ahead, the donkey's lead rope wrapped around his hand. They had to clear the mountain pass before they could find a place to stay for the night.

"Joseph! Another!" Mary cried out.

"I'm here." He kept hold of the rope and ran to Mary's side. He took her hand. "Squeeze my fingers. Hold on!"

She breathed hard, her eyes shut tight. "Pray! Please."

"I will." Joseph steadied her with his other hand. "Father, be with us!" he cried out. "We can't have a baby out here. Please! We need Your help, God. Right now!"

Mary's grip on his hand eased and she slumped against him, clearly worn out. "I'm not sure . . . I can do this."

"You can." He refused to let fear spill into his voice. "God is with us. He knew there would be a census. We have to believe that."

For half a minute Mary didn't move or speak or do anything but hold on to him, her whole body trembling. Then, gradually, she took a few deep breaths and sat up straighter. "The pain's gone. We can keep going." Her lips lifted in a half smile, but her eyes showed her weariness. "I'm ready."

"You're sure?" Joseph would carry her in his arms all the way to Bethlehem if he had to. "You're strong enough?"

"I am." She closed her eyes for a moment. "Just . . . a little dizzy."

Joseph looked at the back of the donkey. "You see the cross? On his back there?" All donkeys had the marking of a large black cross high on their backs. Something they were born with. This one was no exception.

Mary nodded. "I see it. Of course."

"Just focus on the center of the cross and hold on. That way you won't fall."

She did as he said and an hour passed as they climbed the mountain with the rest of the caravan headed to Bethlehem. Joseph could credit only a miracle from God that no more pains seized Mary. She remained well even as Joseph prepared their separate tents. A few campfires burned around them, and Joseph led Mary to one of them where he heated up a pack of smoked fish, some bread, and olives.

On their walk back to their tents, Joseph put his arm around Mary. "How are you?"

"Fine." She smiled up at him. "Really."

"God is good." He felt himself relax a little. If they kept their pace they'd be in Bethlehem in two days. "Maybe we'll make it after all."

"Mmmm." They reached the tents and Mary turned to him. "I like this."

"What?" It was the craziest thing she could've said. "The journey?"

She laughed. "Well, not that." Her eyes

44

held his. "The people around the fire, on the caravan. They don't know us. No one's pointing or . . . whispering."

"Aww, Mary." Joseph took her in his arms. "I'm so sorry. All you've been through . . . I would've done anything to spare you a minute of it."

"I know." She drew back. "I couldn't do this without you, Joseph."

"Come get me if you need me. No matter the hour." He touched the side of her face.

She smiled. "No woman ever loved a man more than I love you."

Mary meant every word. Joseph could see that in her eyes. When he turned in that night — despite the chilly air and two days' travel ahead, despite Mary's delicate condition and every wild uncertainty about the future — he fell asleep filled with joy for one reason.

Mary loved him.

They made it to Bethlehem just in time.

The pains were regular now, close enough that Mary said she knew the baby was coming. After all, she'd just watched her cousin Elizabeth go through childbirth. They had maybe a few hours, but now they had another problem — one Joseph had never expected.

Because of the census, the town was packed. People were setting up tents in the city street. But that would never do for Mary, not in her condition. They made it to the inn and he led Mary on the donkey straight to the front door. A man answered, upset, bothered. "What is it?"

"My wife . . . she's about to have a baby. Please, sir. We need a room."

The man peered around Joseph at Mary. At the same time another pain took hold of her. Joseph ran to her side and held her until it passed. "Sir, please!" he yelled. "We have nowhere to go."

"We're full. The census. Every room in the city is taken." He gave a sad shake of his head and shut the door.

Panic coursed through Joseph. What was he supposed to do? His hands shook as he led the donkey away from the inn. Maybe one of the residents had a spot in his home. Joseph started down the street, knocking at the doorway of each house he came to. And each time he would explain: "My wife is in labor . . . the baby could come anytime. Please . . . can you rent us a room?"

Some people closed the door before Joseph finished speaking. Others suggested neighbors or businesses. But after nearly two hours of searching the answer was the same. There was no room for Mary and Joseph.

Night lay heavy over Bethlehem when Mary cried out louder than before. "I can't do this, Joseph. I can't go another moment. Please."

He ran to her side, but this time she seemed different. Her body and face were tense and she couldn't sit upright. Joseph's heart slammed around in his chest. She couldn't have the baby on the side of the road. Joseph stared at the starry sky and whispered, "God, don't You see us? We need You! Please, Lord!"

At the same moment something caught his attention. A stable in a cave not far from them. A covered room. He gritted his teeth. "Hold on, Mary. I have an idea."

She lay collapsed over the neck of the donkey as Joseph eased the animal across the field toward the stable. He opened the door and stepped inside. Cobwebs stuck to his face and the smell nearly made him gag. A few cows had already entered and were bedded down for the night.

Joseph felt the animals watching him as his eyes adjusted. Then he saw something that might help. An animal trough. A manger. Near it was an area of hay. "This'll work," he muttered to himself. He spread his cloak over the hay and helped Mary to the spot. "How are you?"

She was damp with sweat, her body limp as her eyes met his. "I'm scared. It hurts so much and I —"

Another pain seized her. Joseph knelt by her side and stroked her hair, held her hand. *Help her, God . . . please help her.* Eventually the pain let up, but it was followed by another and another until finally, mercifully, the baby came. His cry filled the stable, strong and healthy. Joseph wrapped Him in the rags from his pack and placed Him in Mary's arms.

Her smile gave him permission to relax for the first time in days. They were in a barn, yes. But the baby was here and He was healthy, and, most of all, Mary was okay. They were going to make it.

"Look at Him. He's beautiful." Mary couldn't take her eyes off the child. "Isn't He beautiful, Joseph?"

"He is." For a long moment they stared at the child. "The Savior of the world lies in your arms. It's more than I can understand."

"Me, too." Their eyes met and a knowing passed between them. In all the world only the two of them knew that hundreds of years of silence had been broken. The Messiah had come and He now lay in the arms of His teenage mother.

For a while Mary rested. Flies buzzed about and the smell hit Joseph again. He lifted his eyes to the cracks in the barn roof and tried to see a glimmer of the night sky. *I believe You, Father. I do. But sometimes I wonder if I've missed something along the way.* He glanced at the manger. A feeding trough? For the King of the world? Bugs and animals and flies? Joseph wasn't sure what he had expected for the child's birth, but he hadn't expected this.

As his silent questions continued, a knock came at the stable door. Mary opened her eyes and Joseph scrambled to his feet. Had someone found them? Were they going to be kicked out of even this lowly barn? Joseph tried to feel strong and brave as he walked to the door.

When he opened it, a new kind of shock came over him. A group of plain shepherd men stood on the other side, their eyes wide with wonder. "The angel told us where to find Him! The Savior has been born! Please, can we see Him?"

"Yes." Chills ran down Joseph's arms. "Yes, you're right. He was born tonight."

The shepherds entered the barn and told of the miraculous thing they'd seen. An angel of the Lord had appeared to them and the glory of the Lord had shone around them.

"To tell you the truth, we were scared to death." One of the shepherds smiled. "But the angel told us not to be afraid. He had good news of great joy for all people." He looked at his buddies. "Even us."

Another shepherd nodded. "He told us where to find the baby. Here . . . in a manger."

The first shepherd was looking at Jesus. "Before long, an entire heavenly host appeared. It was most amazing thing in all our lives." He seemed frozen in place. "We had to come. And now we have to go tell everyone."

The shepherds stayed a little while longer and then they left. Different men from those they'd been that morning.

Alone again, Mary fed Jesus while Joseph watched. "You've never looked more beautiful."

"My heart is full. I can't explain it. Of all the people the angel could've told tonight, he told them. Everyday people." Her eyes welled with tears. "Like us."

"What's happened . . . only God can explain."

"I love you, Joseph." Mary smiled at him.

"Whatever's ahead . . . I can't do it without you."

"I'm here, Mary. I'll never leave." Joseph took her hand in his. Deep in his soul something stirred. He felt a sense of love and protection stronger than any he'd ever felt. "I will never let anything happen to either of you. I will spend my life protecting you, loving you. I promise."

Through the night the promise consumed him, while he kept watch over Mary and Jesus, and while he prayed to his Father in heaven. His prayer was simple and profound: That as long as he drew breath, God would help him protect the woman he loved.

And the Christ child God had entrusted to them both.

The confirmation of God's divine plan continued as the baby Jesus grew. Joseph moved his family out of the stable and into a small house in Bethlehem since Jesus was too little to travel. Money was tight, but Joseph had a few months of savings. Every time Joseph had even the first doubts about God's plan or why He'd chosen Joseph, the Father would send a reminder.

One of those reminders, something Joseph would never forget, came with another knock at the door. This time there were three Magi from the Middle East. They came complete with their wealthy caravans, an entire parade set up outside their home.

The wise men came in and shared their story, and Joseph could only listen in awe and wonder. "We followed a star to the place where you live," one of the men said. "We wanted to see the Messiah, and now we have seen Him."

The men smiled at Jesus, asleep in Mary's arms. "We brought gifts," another man told Joseph.

As long as he lived Joseph would never forget seeing the stately wise men and their entourages gathered at his small house. The sight of the kings on their knees holding gifts for little Jesus. Gifts that brought Joseph and his family the funds they would need to survive.

It was one more reminder.

God really had chosen Joseph and Mary to raise the Savior.

Another reminder came soon after the Magi left Bethlehem. This time an angel warned Joseph in a dream that Jesus was in danger. "Get up," the angel said. "Take the child and His mother and escape to Egypt. Stay there until I tell you, for Herod is going to search for the child to kill Him."

Joseph remembered his prayer — that he

might protect his family. He packed up their belongings and the three of them headed out before sunup. Africa was a long and difficult journey from Bethlehem, but every step of the way Joseph was convinced. This was God's calling on his life. He had been born to protect Mary and Jesus. And so Joseph went.

The horror of what King Herod did to destroy the children of Galilee in the season that followed was unspeakable. Herod had ordered the murder of all baby boys two years old and under. All in a search to destroy Jesus. News reached Mary and Joseph and they dropped to their knees, praying for understanding and comfort for all of Israel.

That night Mary held Jesus as He slept. She looked long into Joseph's eyes. "Thank you. For hearing God's voice. For rescuing us."

Joseph took her hands. He had never loved her more. "You are my life, Mary. You and Jesus. The promise I made to you will remain my purpose as long as I live. But the rescue comes from God alone. Always from Him."

In time King Herod died and Joseph heard the voice of the angel in yet another dream. This time he was told to leave Egypt and settle with Mary and Jesus in Nazareth. Not long after, it was time to take young Jesus to the temple.

The rite of passage for every firstborn son in Israel.

"We'll see Elizabeth and Zechariah and John." Mary was excited about their time together.

When they reached Jerusalem, Joseph stood by and watched as Mary and Elizabeth hugged and talked and cried. The toddlers seemed to connect instantly, as if they'd never spent a day apart. Joseph watched, amazed. The connection between Jesus and John went beyond human understanding. And no wonder. Since John would one day prepare the way for his cousin.

Joseph could hardly wait for all that lay ahead.

One day Mary and Joseph were walking with Jesus in the temple courts when an old holy man approached them. His eyes were bright with the light of the Holy Spirit, and despite the crowd he singled out Mary and Joseph as if he'd known them all his life.

"My name is Simeon," he told Joseph. "Please, may I hold the child?"

Joseph sensed he had nothing to fear from Simeon. He carefully handed Jesus over.

What happened next would stay with Joseph and Mary forever. With Jesus in his arms, the old man stared up at the sky and proclaimed that he could die in peace now because his eyes had seen the salvation come for all people.

Joseph put his arm around Mary and the two of them marveled over Simeon's knowledge — further proof that God was with them, that Jesus truly was His Son. But then, Simeon turned to Mary. His eyes shone with tears, and grief filled his expression.

"This child is destined to cause the falling and rising of many in Israel and to be a sign that will be spoken against — so that the thoughts of many hearts will be revealed." He hesitated, choking on the words as if they were coming to him bit by bit. "I'm sorry." He reached out to Mary. "A sword will pierce your own soul, too."

A soft gasp fell from Mary's lips but she said nothing, gave no response. Joseph took the baby back from Simeon and wished him well. As the man left, Joseph turned to his wife and pulled her into his arms. "Mary, I'm so sorry you had to hear that."

She looked stricken. "What does it mean? A sword will pierce my soul, too?"

"I don't know." Joseph stroked her hair,

the baby Jesus safe between them. "But I'm here. Nothing will harm you or baby Jesus. Nothing." He stood a little straighter. "God gave me this job and I will spend my life doing it." He put his hand on her cheek. "I love you. I will always love you."

"I love you, too." She rested her head on his shoulder.

The crowds passed around them, but Mary and Joseph and Jesus stayed unmoving, huddled together until Mary was ready to move on. As they neared the outer edges of the temple court they were approached again — this time by a prophetess named Anna. The woman was old like Simeon, and like Simeon, she knew Jesus.

Despite the crowd, and all the chaos and confusion, she knew Him.

She touched the child's head and smiled into Mary and Joseph's eyes. "This is the Savior of the world," she whispered. "Thanks be to God for saving His people!" And then with all the happiness of the greatest celebration ever, Anna turned to the crowd around them and shouted with joy, "This is the Savior of the world! Thanks be to God! Thanks to our great and mighty Father!"

The happy moment was another sign from God, reassuring Joseph that all was well and that the Lord was with them.

Both the baby in their keeping, and the Father above.

After that, every year when Joseph took Mary and Jesus to Jerusalem for Passover, Mary would bring up the words of Simeon. And every year Joseph would remind her of his promise. Nothing would happen to the child as long as he was alive.

Nothing.

The Feast of the Passover was important to Joseph, as it was to all those who loved God and followed His ways. It was a time to journey from Nazareth to Jerusalem, a time to meet up with Mary's relatives — Elizabeth and Zechariah and John.

A time to draw closer to the Lord.

Usually Joseph and his family stayed several days before returning home, and that was the case the year Jesus turned twelve. As with every other year, Joseph and Mary and Jesus traveled in a caravan of people trekking to the city for the holiday. The visit and celebration had been wonderful. But they were a day into the journey home when suddenly Mary realized the impossible.

Jesus was not with them.

"I know I saw Him." Mary clung to Joseph, her face filled with fear. "He was with

John when we left. He wouldn't have stayed in Jerusalem, would He?"

Joseph's heart beat hard, his breath jagged and uneven. "We'll find Him. Come on." Together they searched the entire caravan, but Mary was right. Jesus was not with them.

Terrified and begging God for answers, Mary and Joseph turned around and traveled as quickly as they could back to Jerusalem. They found Elizabeth and Zechariah first. Mary's relatives were still in Jerusalem and John was with them. But none of them had seen Jesus.

Three long days passed and finally Joseph was out of answers. Never had he been so scared and confused. This time no angels spoke to him, no strangers came up to them to tell them things they didn't know about their son. He was simply missing.

Finally, on the third day, Joseph ran with Mary to the temple courts and there — sitting among the teachers — was Jesus. From a distance they watched, relieved and frustrated. The teachers seemed mesmerized by Him. He asked questions, but more than that, He provided answers. Tears filled Mary's eyes as she watched their son. "Why would He do this?" she whispered. "Make us worry?"

"Look at Him." Joseph held Mary close, still at a distance from Jesus. "The teachers are amazed at His understanding."

Mary listened quietly. "Yes." Her frightened eyes turned to Joseph's. "But three days?"

Jesus must've known they were there. He finished His conversation and then hurried over.

"Son, why have You treated us like this?" Mary gathered Him in her arms, clearly as relieved as she was upset. "Your father and I have been anxiously searching for You."

Jesus looked from Mary to Joseph and back again. "Why were you searching for Me?" His face looked as innocent as summer. "Didn't you know I had to be in My Father's house?"

The words stabbed at Joseph's heart. Though he loved Jesus with his whole being, this was the first time he truly understood his place. He was Jesus's stepfather. Nothing more. Though Jesus returned with them to Nazareth, and though He remained obedient, His words stayed with Joseph. Never mind the rescue from Bethlehem or Egypt. It didn't matter what Joseph had done to protect Jesus or how much he loved Mary. Forget the reality that Joseph had been there from the beginning. Joseph would never be Jesus's father.

That role belonged to God alone.

"He has a different purpose," Mary said to Joseph one night after they returned to Nazareth. "He does not belong to us. I understand that better now."

"Yes." Joseph pulled her into his arms.

"It scares me, Joseph."

"Me, too." He eased back and looked past her eyes to her heart. "The time is coming when the world will know."

"And when that time comes" — Mary put her hand over her heart — "every moment we have shared with Him will be here. Inside my soul."

"And you, Mary." He kissed her forehead. "You will forever be in mine."

Joseph did what he could, raising the Savior, loving His mother, picking wild orchids for Mary when she needed a reason to smile. Some seasons and years he felt too small for the task. Not brave enough or wise enough or strong enough. But then Joseph would remember the journey to Bethlehem or the one to Egypt. The times when Jesus was too small and Mary too weak. God had chosen him to protect the Savior and His mother back then, and Joseph would continue to do so as long as the Lord allowed.

The years blended, one into another, and Jesus grew strong. The townspeople knew Him and loved Him. He helped Joseph in the carpenter's shop and He cared for Mary better than any son in Nazareth. He was the best big brother their other boys could've hoped for.

When Joseph began to cough late one winter, Jesus took on most of the work.

"I'll be fine," Joseph told Jesus one morning. "But until I recover, I need You, son. Thank You for Your help."

Jesus promised to do anything He could, and while He took over in the carpenter's shop, Mary tended to Joseph.

"You're so thin." Mary sat at his bedside, fear in her eyes. "Your cough sounds worse."

"I'll be fine." He held out his hand. "Stay by me, Mary. You make me feel well again. I think I'm getting better."

Instead, as the days passed, Joseph grew worse. Finally it became clear that their prayers would not be answered with a healing. The miracle would be something else, something still to come.

"I don't want you to go." Tears spilled down Mary's cheeks as she sat with him late one afternoon. "I can't live without you, Joseph. You're the only one who really knows me."

61

"My love." Joseph struggled to his feet and held Mary until he could no longer stand. "I will be with you always. In your heart. Remember?"

The sobs came over her, making it impossible for her to speak. But her eyes said everything her words could not. Soon people would know their Son. He was the Messiah. But no one would know Him the way Mary and Joseph had. No one would share a bond as intimate as theirs.

Joseph's eyes fell on the small prayer table, the one he had made for Mary before they received news about Jesus. Their marriage had not been what they had planned. The simple life, the small-town existence and normal family they had imagined never materialized.

But what they did have was richer than life.

That night Joseph grew weaker still and finally he asked for Jesus. With Mary at one side of his bed and Jesus at the other, Joseph turned his eyes to his oldest Son. "Your time is coming, Jesus."

"Yes." Jesus took hold of Joseph's hands. "And yours."

Joseph nodded. His life was slipping away. He could feel it. He looked at Mary, at the love of his life, and then back to Jesus.

"Please . . . take care of her. She needs You."

"You have My word." Jesus's eyes filled with tears. "You have done everything right. You were the best earthly father I could've had." He reached across the bed and took Mary's hand. "Don't worry. As long as I am alive I will care for My mother." Sadness and finality hung in the air around them. "I'll see that she is cared for . . . if it's the last thing I do."

With that, a peace filled Joseph such as he'd never known before. He turned his eyes to Mary. "My love . . ." His vision blurred with tears. "How have the years gone so quickly? I don't want to leave you."

"You never will." She leaned close and held him. "I will keep you with me, Joseph. Every kind thing you've ever done. Every loving word and moment."

"We will be together again one day."

"And all our questions will be answered."

Joseph could feel his heart slowing, his breathing growing more shallow. He nodded and managed the slightest smile. He wished he could have one more day, to walk along the hillside out back and pick wild orchids for Mary. As he'd done so many times before. But he was leaving her. He couldn't stop it. As darkness closed in around him, he didn't look away. The last thing he saw this side of heaven was the thing he loved most in all the world.

His beloved Mary.

STORY 2
ZECHARIAH
THE KNOWING UNCLE

Zechariah's prayer never changed.

Sure, he sought God often and for many reasons. As a priest, he prayed for the people of Israel and for his hometown in the hill country of Judea. He prayed for God to break His silence to their nation and for the Lord's faithfulness to the Jewish people. But one prayer never changed.

The prayer that he and his wife, Elizabeth, might have a child.

Sure, they were old compared to most people having children. Their friends had been in their late teens and early twenties when they welcomed children. He and Elizabeth were in their mid-thirties. But Zechariah refused to give up hope. Children were still a possibility for them. They weren't as old as Abraham and Sarah, after all. But still, they were on the other side of fertility. Most of their peers were done with child-rearing, ready to welcome grandchildren.

Never mind that. Zechariah was nothing if not faithful. As long as God gave him the ability to pray, he would ask for a miracle.

For the child he had longed for all his married life.

Zechariah placed his bag on the bed and filled it with enough clothes and food for the week's journey. This was Passover week, and he was one of hundreds of priests reporting to Jerusalem for his temple duties. He was nearly finished packing when he took a break and looked out back. There was Elizabeth working in their garden. Faithful, beautiful, tender-hearted Elizabeth.

Their names held a promise that other people might have given up on long ago. Zechariah's name meant "The Lord has remembered." Elizabeth's meant "My God has sworn an oath." Zechariah stared at his beautiful wife. So how was it that two people who loved the Lord, two people named for His faithfulness, were barren this late in life?

Zechariah had no answers.

He sighed. "Maybe this time, God." He whispered the words from the depths of his soul. "Maybe this time You will hear my prayers."

He finished packing and joined his wife

outside. She was gathering leafy greens from a spot set aside for vegetables, but she looked lost in thought. "Elizabeth, darling." He came up alongside her, laying his hand on her shoulder. "What are you thinking?"

"About your trip." Her smile was weary, but it came all the same. "It always stirs hope in me. Whenever you go to the temple."

"Hmm." He smiled at her. "For me, too."

"Miracles happen at the temple." Again she smiled, erasing some of the weariness in her eyes. "At least I want to believe they do."

"Maybe this will be the year." Zechariah didn't have to say for what. They both knew.

"Yes, my love." She reached for his hand and for a long moment their eyes held. "Maybe so."

Long after Zechariah and Elizabeth were in for the night, the thought stayed with him. Maybe this was the time. He believed it as strongly as she did. The two of them always believed. But that hadn't made the years any easier.

Before Zechariah fell asleep he felt himself going back, back to the early days of his marriage to Elizabeth. The days when they first found out she was barren. Elizabeth came from a line of priests — same as Zechariah. Elizabeth was from the line of Aaron, and Zechariah from the line of Abijah. Their families' hopes for their marriage were surpassed only by their own.

In those early days, Zechariah could see the future as easily as the sunrise. They would have a house full of children, girls like Elizabeth and sons to carry on the line of priestly duties. There would be laughter and long walks, the joy of happy children in their home, and a purpose of raising the next generation for God.

But life hadn't played out that way. One year became two and soon five years had passed without a child. About that time they started getting looks from their neighbors. Their families began asking questions. "What's the problem?" Zechariah's father asked him one night. "You two should have several children by now."

Zechariah never knew what to say. Not to his father or to Elizabeth's father. Not to the local priests — all of whom were as concerned as Zechariah. The inability to have children made them pariahs in town, people to be avoided. Social outcasts.

One day not long after their seventh anniversary, Zechariah was working at his desk when he heard something in the next room. He followed the sound and there he found

Elizabeth. She was crying, her hands over her face. Zechariah went to her and helped her gently to her feet. "What is it? Has someone hurt you?"

"No." She was clearly trying to find control over her emotions, but she could not. "What have I done? Why won't God give me a baby?"

Zechariah felt her frustration. "God is faithful. I know that." He held her close. "Why He has kept children from our home, I don't know."

"I would be a good mother, Zechariah. I would hold my babies and love them. I would raise them to know our God."

"Of course you would." Zechariah had never felt more helpless.

"People look at me when I walk down the street. As if I've done something wrong."

"You've done nothing. It isn't that." He smoothed her hair back from her face and searched her eyes. "We must keep praying. That one day — like our families and friends — we will also know the joy of having a baby."

Eventually the tears stopped and Elizabeth agreed with him. They would keep praying. What else could they do? And so it went, year after year after year.

Now they'd been married nearly twenty

summers. Anyone who had looked at them with a wary eye had long since lost interest. The rest of their town figured it would never happen. Only Zechariah and Elizabeth believed a miracle was still possible. Only the two of them still prayed for God to bring them a child.

And there was no better time to raise their voices to God again than now — Passover. When Zechariah would make the short trek to Jerusalem with hundreds of priests to do the temple duties. The trip left Zechariah and Elizabeth feeling the same every time.

Maybe this was the year.

Zechariah set out at dawn the next day.

This time nearly five hundred priests were heading to the temple. From the hour he set out with his priestly division, Zechariah felt different. He could sense the presence of God, and for the first time in many years he let go of his discouragement about being childless.

His work as a priest was his purpose, his calling. He would take the trip to Jerusalem with an expectant heart. However God wanted to use him, Zechariah was ready.

As their division reached the city, a rush of familiar sights and sounds greeted them. The temple area was alive with commerce, congested with locals and tourists come for the Passover. People bustled about, anxious to make their way into the courts to sacrifice and atone for their sins. The temple courts stayed busy year-round, but this was the busiest season of all. People were more mindful of their dependence on God, their expectancy of Him.

The priests knew the routine. Each day for seven days they would gather in a spot near the temple courts where lots would be drawn. The process left little to the imagination. After centuries of tradition, the temple ways had long since been established. Each morning four lots would be chosen — each representing a different temple job.

The priest who drew the first lot would prepare the altar for the burnt offering. This was a functional task, clearing the ashes from the previous offering and laying fresh wood for the current sacrifice. The priest who picked the second lot would slay the sacrificial lamb and the fourth priest chosen by lot would arrange the pieces of the sacrifice on the altar.

Everyone knew the third lot was the most important.

The third lot would go to the priest responsible for offering incense on the altar, in the temple itself. The incense wasn't what caused the third lot to be so important. It was what the incense represented. For the Jewish people, the rich aroma represented prayer. The offering of incense in the holiest Holy Place was the most profound moment of Israel's worship — day and night for hundreds of years.

Zechariah thought about all this as the priests assembled the first morning. A priest might go his whole life and never be called to one of the temple duties. Only a small number would ever receive the third lot.

So as they gathered that day, Zechariah tried to hold on to his hope. He believed God had a plan — for His people, and for Zechariah and Elizabeth. But as he looked around he felt less worthy than any of them. The other priests had families — daughters and sons to carry on their lineage and bring them joy. He could think of no reason why God would bless him and his wife this time.

He could almost feel the others — his peers of many years — looking at him with disdain. The priest without children. He glanced at the eyes of the priests on either side of him, those across from him. He could practically hear their thoughts. *Old Zechariah. Childless. He must've done something wrong. He'll never draw a lot. Not Zechariah.*

He closed his eyes. *God, clear my head. If I've disobeyed You, show me. But save me from these doubts. Thank You, Father.* Zechariah exhaled and opened his eyes. The box was being passed around. Only four lots were marked. The first one went to Levi from the tribe of Jesse. A little farther down the line, Matthew drew a lot. He was from the tribe of Simeon.

Zechariah watched closely, holding his breath as the box came his way. Then, with great reverence and unwarranted hope, he made his choice. His own gasp was the first he heard. But it was hardly the last. The whispers were instant.

The third lot had gone to Zechariah.

Zechariah, of all the priests. The one from the hill country of Judea. The one without children. Zechariah's hands trembled. Had this really happened? Had God allowed him to draw the third lot? His mouth felt dry and he couldn't move for the first minute. The box was still being passed around and soon the fourth lot was drawn.

First day of Passover and the priests had been chosen. Next to him, one of the men leaned close. "Shalom! Good for you, Zechariah." The priest gave him a congratulatory pat on the back. "The Lord has blessed you." A few other men expressed their happiness for Zechariah. But most stayed silent.

Zechariah lifted his face, the heat of the morning sun on his cheeks. Never mind what anyone thought. God had chosen him to offer the incense. The responsibility was tremendous. That alone consumed his thoughts as he walked with the other chosen priests toward the temple.

For a moment he wished Elizabeth could see him. She would be so proud, so happy. Zechariah went to the Holy of Holies, the place where the incense was kept, and for a long time he waited, letting his worldly thoughts leave, focusing his attention on God alone.

Finally the time came, and with great reverence Zechariah entered the Most Holy Place. He set the incense on the altar and carefully lit it. The smoke curled into the air slowly, reverently. A serene sense of holiness filled Zechariah, a feeling he'd never known before. He stared at the holy place, at the burning incense. A different priest would be in this same spot tonight, the way priests had stood here 730 times a year. Year after year after year. Priests had come and would always come to this place to burn incense, bringing to God the prayers of the people and presenting the Lord an offering of praise.

Their heavenly Father had been silent for many long centuries. Zechariah's eyes stayed locked on the incense. Would today be any different? He mustered up his determination. Yes, today would be different. For this was *his* turn to come before God. Other priests might be more blessed, but Zechariah loved God. He definitely loved Him. That love welled up in him as he spread his hands and cried out to God. The requests were similar, but each priest prayed in his own way.

"Father, I am not worthy to stand here in Your presence, but I come to You out of obedience. You allowed me to choose the third lot and so I am here to pray for the people. God, remember Your people, be faithful to the covenants You've made, those promises sworn to our forefathers. Hear us and heal our land. Show mercy to Your people. And selfishly I beg You for a child, for a baby even in our later years when —"

Suddenly from out of nowhere came a flash of light. Zechariah blinked and there at the right side of the altar of incense stood a man in shining white. Fear gripped Zechariah and he could barely breathe. Should he run or scream or drop to his knees? And who was the man? Zechariah was still deciding when the stranger opened his mouth and began to speak.

"Do not be afraid, Zechariah. Your prayer has been heard."

Wonder and awe filled him. The man had to be an angel, sent from God. His message was too great to comprehend. Zechariah's prayers for the people of Israel had been heard. Before he could absorb the words, the angel opened his mouth again. "Your wife, Elizabeth, will bear you a son, and you are to call him John."

Zechariah wondered if he might collapse to the ground and never get up. Not only had his prayers for the people of Israel been heard, but God had also heard Zechariah's most intimate prayers, the ones closest to his heart. The ones he had cried out to God every day since he and Elizabeth married. The prayer that they might have a child.

The angel shone like the sun at midday as he continued to speak. "John will be a joy and delight to you, and many will rejoice because of his birth, for he will be great in the sight of the Lord."

Zechariah felt tears in his eyes. He was going to have a son! And not just any son, but one who would be great in the sight of the Lord! It took all Zechariah's concentration to focus. The angel was still speaking. It was too soon to celebrate.

"John is never to take wine or other fermented drink, and he will be filled with the Holy Spirit, even from birth." The angel hesitated, as if the next part might be most important of all. "He will bring many of the people of Israel back to the Lord their God. And he will go on before the Lord, in the spirit and power of Elijah, to turn the hearts of the fathers to their children and the disobedient to the wisdom of the righteous — to make ready a people prepared for the Lord."

What? The pronouncement swirled in his heart and soul. Zechariah could no longer feel his feet beneath him. This news from the angel was more than he could take. Had he heard correctly? His son was going to prepare the way for the Lord? He had always believed, always prayed. Even when others would've long given up, Zechariah held out hope. But the idea that his son might be a modern-day Elijah?

Zechariah wasn't sure whether to laugh or cry.

Hope and joy practically lifted him off the ground and his smile had never been bigger. The barren days were behind them. Elizabeth was going to have a baby! He blinked, trying to take in everything the angel had said. But even as he rejoiced, reality settled in around him. Was he only dreaming? Could the figure before him really be an angel? He and Elizabeth were too old. What would the neighbors think? And what if he was only imagining everything that had just happened? What if he was only carried away by the excitement of burning the incense?

Maybe he was celebrating too quickly. Dreaming up the moment.

Yes, that had to be it. Nothing the angel had told him was even a little bit possible. Zechariah felt his disbelief gaining ground. He leaned against the nearest wall, his eyes squinty with doubt. "How can I be sure of this?" He took a step closer. "I am an old man and my wife is well along in years."

The angel of the Lord stood taller, his eyes blazing. "I am Gabriel. I stand in the presence of God, and I have been sent to speak to you and to tell you this good news."

Authority rang from the angel's voice and Zechariah felt the wind being sucked from his lungs. The angel continued, "And now . . . now you will be silent and not able to speak until the day this happens." His stern expression left no doubt as to the seriousness of the moment. "Because you did not believe my words, which will come true at their appointed time."

Zechariah wanted to apologize. He wanted to explain his doubts and the years of unanswered prayers. He wasn't crazy to have a few questions, right? About how Elizabeth might have a child now, after all this time? He wanted to ask the angel a hundred things, like, was this the same angel Gabriel who visited Daniel? Zechariah wasn't sure where to start. But when he opened his mouth to speak, not a sound came out.

He had been silenced — just as the angel said. And like that, the angel Gabriel — in all his glory and profound declaration — was gone. Zechariah put his hand to his throat and tried again. Nothing. No sounds, no words. He couldn't speak at all. Which could mean only one thing.

Everything the angel had said was true.

Zechariah raised his hands high and dropped to his knees before the altar of incense. There, in utter praise and worship, a song began to form in his heart. A song to the great God and Father of the universe, who had heard his prayers and sent the angel of the Lord. The God who had chosen him to raise up the little boy who would one day prepare the people for the Savior.

There was no telling how long Zechariah stayed there, silently praising God and reliving his time with the angel Gabriel. Finally, he needed to leave, needed to face the public. More time had passed than usual, so when Zechariah walked out of the temple, a crowd had gathered.

He opened his mouth to speak, but of course no sound came from him. *The angel was serious,* he thought. *I won't be able to talk until the baby comes.* Even still he tried to communicate with the crowd. He pointed to his throat and opened his mouth — showing them that he could not talk. Then he did his best to act out what had happened — how he'd been praying on behalf of the people when an angel had appeared to him.

The people watched, curious. But none of them seemed to understand what had happened. "He's seen a vision!" one man cried out. "He must've seen a vision in the temple!"

Zechariah pointed to the man, jumping around so everyone would know that he had indeed seen something remarkable in the temple. The one time he had truly wonderful news to tell and he couldn't speak! Zechariah finally gave up. The people would know one day. Not just those in attendance in the temple courts that morning.

But all people, everywhere.

■ ■ ■ ■

Zechariah had never been more excited to see Elizabeth. After the priestly duties of the week were fulfilled, he hurried home with his division. The moment his front door came into view he ran toward it and flew inside to find his wife.

She must've seen in his face that something had happened. Something big. Her cheeks grew pale and taut and she took hold of his arm. "Zechariah, what is it? What happened?"

He tried to talk, but of course not a sound came from him.

"You can't talk! Zechariah, what happened in the city? I've never seen you like this."

Zechariah forced himself to be calm. He couldn't get any message across by mouthing words in frantic excitement. Instead he looked deep into her eyes and then tenderly he placed his hand on her flat stomach. For a long time he didn't move, didn't do anything but look to the deepest places of Elizabeth's heart.

She glanced down at his hand and then back at him. "You're praying about our baby? Is that it?"

He shook his head. He could hardly be frustrated with her. It was his fault he couldn't talk, his doubts that had caused the trouble he was in. He held up his pointer finger and thought quickly. There had to be a way to communicate with her. He remembered the scrolls he kept in the far corner of the house. He used them for Bible study, but certainly he could use one to talk to her.

Gesturing to Elizabeth that he'd be right back, he ran and found a single scroll and a reed pen. He couldn't write much, since scrolls weren't easy to come by. But he had to explain the situation. He hurried back to Elizabeth. Then he scribbled out the essential part of the message, the part that mattered most of all: *God . . . sent . . . an . . . angel.*

His next words were the happiest ones he'd ever shared with her. *You're going to have a baby.*

"What?" She put her hand to her face. "Zechariah! A baby? After all these years?" A soft gasp came from Elizabeth. She went to him and he set down the scroll and pen. He took her in his arms. They stood that way for a long time until Zechariah could feel Elizabeth's quiet tears through his garment. "I'm going to have a baby." She looked up at him. "What about your voice?"

Once more he scribbled the words. *I didn't believe. I'll speak when the baby comes.*

"You didn't believe the angel?" Compassion and grace flooded Elizabeth's eyes. "Why, my love?"

Zechariah wanted nothing more than to assure her that he believed now. He wanted to share every detail and moment, every word. But all he could do was capture the story in bits and pieces. He smiled at her and ran his hand along her hair. Then he picked up the scroll and pen again.

It took time, but gradually Zechariah was able to communicate most of the story to his wife. God had heard their prayers. The baby would be a prophet, sent to point the people to the Lord, the Messiah. The One foretold. He would be a wonderful boy, filled with the Holy Spirit from birth. And he would turn the hearts of the people of Israel back to God.

Elizabeth looked as if she might faint from joy and wonder as Zechariah struggled through the story. *A song is building in my heart,* he wrote. *I'll sing it one day.*

He saved the most important detail for last. Zechariah wrote each word with the greatest care and emphasis: *He . . . must . . . be . . . called . . . John.*

"John?" Elizabeth's smile faded slightly. "There's no one in our family by that name."

Zechariah shook his head. He had to make himself very clear — especially on this detail. He found an open area on the scroll and wrote with more fervor this time. *His name is John.* Zechariah pointed at the name. He hoped Elizabeth could see the sincerity in his eyes.

"Okay." She looked down at the rough paper. "I don't understand, but I believe you. His name will be John."

For the first time since the angel's appearance, peace washed over Zechariah's heart. Despite his initial reaction, he had explained the angel's visit to his wife and now they both believed. They believed with all their hearts because nothing was impossible with God.

Not even this.

The next five months were quiet — for both Zechariah and Elizabeth. Sure enough, she became pregnant right after his return from the temple, and from the beginning she decided to stay removed from the townspeople.

"I want this time just for us," she explained one afternoon. She put her hand

84

over her belly. "This miracle is from God. People will know in time. Until then let's keep it between just us."

Zechariah could only agree. After all, he still couldn't talk. And since he had been the one to see the angel, Elizabeth would have a more difficult time explaining things to the neighbors.

At the start of Elizabeth's last trimester, they were sitting at the table one afternoon when a knock sounded at the door. Zechariah answered it and there — breathless and filled with awe — was Elizabeth's young cousin Mary. Immediately she ran to Elizabeth.

"Greetings, my dear cousin!" Mary hugged her and then searched her eyes. "The angel said you were going to have a baby! I had to come see for myself."

Suddenly Elizabeth's hand flew to her stomach and she let out a sound that was more laugh than cry. Zechariah watched from across the room and saw something different in his wife. Her eyes took on a deeper look of serenity. As if the moment Mary walked into the house Elizabeth had somehow changed.

Elizabeth stood and hugged Mary. Then in a knowing voice she proclaimed, "Blessed are you among women!" She took Mary's hand and spoke straight to her. "And blessed is the child you will bear! But why am I so favored, that the mother of my Lord should come to me?"

Now it was Mary's turn to react. She lifted her face to the heavens and whispered a prayer of thanks to God. She looked again at Elizabeth. "Then you know?"

"Yes." Elizabeth's eyes shone with an unearthly wonder. "I know now."

For a moment neither of the women said anything.

Across the room Zechariah was as shocked as his wife. The miracle God was doing didn't involve only their unborn son, John, it involved Mary and her unborn baby, too. More than that, Mary was carrying the Lord. The Savior of the world. Zechariah looked around. It was as if they were all standing on holy ground.

Elizabeth looked at Mary again, and this time tears brimmed in her eyes. She repeated the words she'd said earlier, this time in a whisper. "But why am I so favored, that the mother of my Lord should come to me?"

"The angel Gabriel told me about your baby. He said that nothing was impossible with God. I thought you might help me know how to do this. If I stayed a while."

"That's right." Elizabeth drew a calming

breath and once more she put her hand over her rounded belly. "As soon as the sound of your greeting reached my ears, the baby in my womb leaped for joy." Elizabeth turned back and looked at her husband for a few seconds. Then she returned her eyes to Mary. "Stay with us, Mary. I've been a midwife for two decades. I will show you all I know about having a child." She smiled. "Blessed is she who has believed that what the Lord has said to her will be accomplished."

Zechariah watched the women. Clearly, the plan playing out was bigger than they had known. Their baby John's cousin was going to be the Savior. The Messiah. And their son John would prepare the way. Zechariah would regret forever not believing the angel from the beginning. But this much he knew for sure: Whatever happened now they would believe it together. As a family.

With the beautiful words from Elizabeth, tears spilled on Mary's cheeks. She took hold of both Elizabeth's hands and began to sing. It was a song similar to the one growing in Zechariah's heart — a song of praise and worship to God for what He was doing.

"My soul glorifies the Lord and my spirit rejoices in God my Savior," Mary sang. "For

He has been mindful of the humble state of His servant."

Zechariah wouldn't have been surprised to see Gabriel show up here, too. The moment felt that sacred.

Mary kept singing, filling the home with truth and prophecy: "From now on all generations will call me blessed, for the Mighty One has done great things for me — holy is His name."

She kept singing about the mercy of God and His mighty deeds, how He scattered those who were proud — even rulers. "He has filled the hungry with good things, but has sent the rich away empty." Her eyes glistened as she finished her song.

For a long time neither of the women said anything. Zechariah held on to the words of Mary's melody, the way each line seemed to come from God. He couldn't forget the part about His filling the hungry with good things.

Mary hugged Elizabeth again and then she began to tell in detail about the angel's visit. "I haven't told Joseph yet. I'm not sure . . . how he'll react."

"He may struggle." Elizabeth patted Mary's hand. "But God is at the center of this." She looked at Zechariah. "For all of us." Again her eyes turned to Mary. "He will make all things clear even to Joseph. He will."

"You're right." Mary's eyes didn't look troubled. "I need to trust God. It's just . . . I love Joseph so much."

"And he loves you." Again Elizabeth looked back and smiled at Zechariah. "We both will pray when the time comes for you to tell him."

Zechariah tried to imagine how Joseph would feel. His betrothed would return home with news that she was pregnant. Zechariah had struggled to believe an angel. The task ahead of Joseph was far more difficult than that, and so yes, they would pray.

They would pray as never before.

Mary stayed for three months. Not only was she a comfort to Elizabeth as her pregnancy finished, but Zechariah enjoyed watching her learn along the way.

Zechariah would come into the room and often catch Elizabeth sharing details of the birthing process with Mary, what she had to look forward to, which parts would be most difficult. Mary stayed with Elizabeth and Zechariah until John's birth. Elizabeth wanted Mary to experience the actual delivery. So she could show her what to do when the time came for her baby to be born.

Her Jesus. The Savior of the World.

Every day Zechariah would listen to the women and pray to God. As he did, the song in his heart continued to grow and swell. By the time Elizabeth entered her final month of pregnancy it was a song Zechariah knew by heart — a song of joy and praise to God for His faithfulness. Not only to Zechariah and Elizabeth.

But to all the nation of Israel.

Finally Elizabeth's time drew near. Mary was ready now to help with the delivery — and in the process learn firsthand what lay ahead for her. Even in that, Zechariah marveled at God's faithfulness, how He hadn't missed a single detail.

Every day Zechariah wished for a voice so he could offer words of encouragement and help to his precious wife. He could look in her eyes, but he couldn't voice how happy he was for this moment, the one they had prayed and waited for these past twenty years. Their son was about to be born!

The hours blended one into another and Elizabeth's pains grew stronger, closer together. Then from the other room Zechariah heard his wife cry out. Seconds later he heard the wailing of their healthy baby boy. Zechariah had wondered if he might regain his voice the moment the child arrived. But he remained unable to speak. After a short time, Zechariah joined his wife and still he could not comment. Not on the beauty of the baby or the joy in his heart or the miracle he felt as he held his son for the first time.

"He's amazing, isn't he?" Elizabeth took the child from Zechariah. "He's the most beautiful baby ever."

Mary stood with them, tears in her eyes. "Your precious John . . . He is a miracle." She put her hand over her still-flat stomach. "Our sons will change the world."

"God's redemption begins today." Elizabeth smiled at Mary and then kissed her baby's cheek. "Hello, John . . . sweet baby. Hello! God has big plans for you."

It nearly killed Zechariah not to add his voice to those of Elizabeth and Mary. But again he let his eyes do the talking. He spent as many hours as he could holding John and rocking him, staring into his face and wondering about the things this child would do in years to come. How would he prepare the way for the Lord? What would that look like? The future would certainly be very bright indeed — especially for their John.

Zechariah could only thank God that he and Elizabeth were chosen to be the boy's parents. Surely goodness and mercy would follow all of them for the rest of their days. Nobody's future looked as bright as theirs.

Mary waited until the baby was a few days old before she left for Nazareth. Zechariah stood by as Elizabeth prayed with Mary before she left, that Joseph would understand the news and that he would believe the truth about the baby. "Please keep praying that he'll believe me." Mary's face was filled with hope. "My story . . . it will be hard to understand."

"Remember what the angel told you." Elizabeth smiled. She had John in her arms and was surrounded by a serenity that only added to her beauty. "Nothing is impossible with God."

"Thank you." Mary nodded, and peace seemed to come over her again. "I will hold on to that truth every day."

They hugged again and then Mary was gone.

Over the next few days, their neighbors and family members stopped by the house often. They understood that the Lord had shown Elizabeth and Zechariah great mercy. Together they celebrated the goodness and faithfulness of God.

When the eighth day came, John was circumcised and various family members stepped forward. It was time to name the baby boy. Since Zechariah couldn't speak, many of them declared the child's name to be Zechariah — after his father, the priest.

Elizabeth hurried to them and shook her head. "No, his name is not Zechariah." She smiled at her husband. "He is to be called John."

The family members looked from one to the other, confused. "There isn't a single relative with that name, Elizabeth. Let's ask Zechariah. He will know what to do."

"What should he be called, Zechariah?" one of his older uncles asked. "He ought to be named after you."

Zechariah felt his heart rate double. He hurried and found a scroll.

With all the room watching, he wrote: *His . . . name . . . is . . . John.*

As he finished the last letter of his son's name, suddenly his tongue was loosed. He could feel it. And just like that he could talk. His words came in a rush of praise to the God who had given them one miracle after another.

Zechariah raised his hands to the Father. "Praise God in the heavens! He alone is worthy to be praised, for He is faithful. All glory and honor and power belong to Him!"

One of their neighbors fell to his knees

and pointed to little John. "Tell us, Zechariah! What do you know of this child?"

A smile came over Zechariah. "He will be a prophet, sent to prepare the way for the Messiah!" His words filled the house, and the people. One at a time family and friends came to Zechariah, hugging him and kissing his cheeks, proclaiming the miracle at hand.

They did the same to Elizabeth and a sense of wonder filled the house. "We have seen a miracle!" several of them shouted, and together the people in the house praised God.

Once the room quieted, the family and friends turned to Zechariah. "What has happened? Tell us!"

The song that had been building and growing in Zechariah's heart came to life and he felt himself being filled with the presence of God. The feeling grew and finally Zechariah could do nothing but sing. He stood at the front of the room, a smile stretched across his face, and sang as if all his life had led to this moment.

"Praise be to the Lord the God of Israel, because He has come and has redeemed His people. He has raised up a horn of salvation for us in the house of His servant David — as He said through His holy prophets long ago — salvation from our enemies and from the hand of all who hate us . . . to show mercy to our fathers and to remember His holy covenant, the oath He swore to our father Abraham."

The people stared at him, swept away by the song. Zechariah understood their shock. This was not his usual way — singing in front of an entire room full of people. This song expressed all that was in Zechariah's heart while he couldn't speak. It was the explanation Elizabeth and the others had been waiting for.

Zechariah continued to sing. ". . . to rescue us from the hand of our enemies, and to enable us to serve Him without fear in holiness and righteousness all our days."

At that, Zechariah felt tears in his eyes. He walked closer to Elizabeth and very carefully he took baby John in his arms. He kissed his son's cheek and his forehead. The rest of the song he sang to the baby alone — as if he had forgotten everyone else in the room.

"And you, my child, will be called a prophet of the Most High; for you will go on before the Lord to prepare the way for him, to give his people the knowledge of salvation through the forgiveness of their sins." Zechariah looked intently at baby

John, his miracle child, his son. "Because of the tender mercy of our God, by which the rising sun will come to us from heaven, to shine on those living in darkness . . . and in the shadow of death, to guide our feet into the path of peace."

Zechariah struggled with that last part of the song. It felt jarring to sing about death now. His baby was so new, so alive and innocent and trusting. The weight and warmth of John sleeping in Zechariah's arms even in this moment brought a comfort he had never known. Whether God had given him those words about Mary's Jesus or about John, Zechariah couldn't be sure. But he clung to the promise all the same.

Because of John and Jesus, people would have hope and guidance — even in the shadow of death.

Even more, they would have peace.

Perfect peace.

John grew and became strong — in spirit and body. He was a model son, helping Elizabeth when it was time to fix a meal and learning from Zechariah what it meant to be a priest. He was kind to the neighbor kids and he especially loved the times every year when Mary and Joseph would bring Jesus and their other children over during

Passover.

Jesus and John had a special connection — one that Zechariah knew would become more profound in years to come. God Himself had told them that through the message of the angel Gabriel. They laughed at the same things and were easily the leaders among their peers. Sometimes John would be upset after Jesus and His family left. "Jesus is my best friend."

"Yes, my boy." Zechariah would only look thoughtfully at his son. "And you are His. I have no doubt about that."

Every day Zechariah thanked God for the joy John brought to their home, and the delight he was in their lives. Zechariah and John often held long conversations out back, studying the sky and stars and handiwork of God's creation. Zechariah had only one wish, one prayer as John grew and the calendar pages turned.

That God would slow the time.

Each year, the night before John's birthday, Zechariah and Elizabeth would wait until John was asleep. Then they'd quietly step into his room and pray over him — holding on to the boy he'd been at five or six or seven years old . . . as long as they could. Some moments Zechariah wanted only to stop the sun from setting — so they could enjoy John a little longer.

But time passed, and Zechariah could do nothing to change it. The night before John's twelfth birthday, Zechariah and Elizabeth prayed over him. Then they had a quiet conversation in the next room.

"It's time." Zechariah could already feel the tears in his eyes. "John needs to go to school. He needs to learn the ways of the Torah."

"You've taught him." Elizabeth surely knew it was time for their son to leave, but like Zechariah she was desperate for a way out. "He only just came into our lives. And now he has to go."

"He'll be home during breaks." Zechariah pulled Elizabeth into his arms and held her. "But we must do our part so he can fulfill his purpose. His calling."

In all his and Elizabeth's lives there had been no greater pleasure than the joy of raising John. But with his twelfth birthday, they could only do what God had asked them to do: release John to the care of teachers in a remote part of the desert. The place where he could best hear God's voice. Young Jewish boys from the priestly orders were traditionally sent away to school so they could learn under the tutelage of rabbis. This had been the way for centuries, and the path would be no different for John.

Especially John.

Elizabeth prepared their son's things and the day before he was to leave, Zechariah called him close. "John, my son, let's take a walk. I want to talk with you before you leave."

"Yes, Father. I want to talk to you, too." John was rugged and handsome, an athletic boy who loved being outdoors. He was excited about the journey to his school and the adventure ahead. But Zechariah could tell the boy was also sad about leaving.

The two of them set out across the dusty ground, beyond the house where John had been raised. Zechariah put his arm around John's shoulders. The boy had grown some but he hadn't gained the height he would when he became a man. For now he was a foot shorter than Zechariah, his voice still that of a child. Zechariah smiled at the boy. "Are you nervous?"

John squinted his eyes against the setting sun. "Sometimes." He managed the slightest grin. "I'll miss you and Mother."

"We'll always be here." Zechariah hid the ache in his heart. "Whenever you have time, you can come home. Your mother and I will be waiting."

"Thank you." John looked at the distant

stream that ran from the oasis behind their house. "Let's walk over there. That's my favorite spot."

"Mine, too." Zechariah and John walked easily together and when they reached the stream, they sat on a large rock. "The teachers at your school are the best in the country." Zechariah smiled. "I went to school with some of them many years ago."

"I want to learn." John stared at the place where the ground and water met. "But I won't know anyone."

"They will know you. Your purpose." Zechariah patted John's knee. "We've talked about this since you were little. You will prepare the way for the Lord. You've been filled with God's Spirit since birth." He smiled at his boy. "You know all these things."

"Yes." John scrunched up his face, focusing intently on the idea. "I believe all of that." He grinned. "Your old friends — my teachers — they prayed for my coming. Just as they prayed for the Messiah to come." He stared at the stream. "Father, do you ever just *feel* something?"

Zechariah thought about the trip to the temple before the visit from the angel Gabriel. How strongly he had felt that God was up to something. "Yes. I have."

"That's how I feel about the water." John picked up a small rock and tossed it in the flowing stream. "I've always been drawn to it. I think the Lord will use water in my life when I'm older. I just have a sense."

A twinge of anxiety passed through Zechariah. If John felt that way about water, he was no doubt right. Of course he would have divine thoughts about his future. But his son's words only reminded Zechariah that the time had come to let go.

The boy's purpose was not here at home but yet ahead.

Zechariah felt his sorrow well up inside him. He could see a tapestry of highlights from John's life, his first steps and first laugh and first words. Tears filled his eyes. He waited until his emotions were under control and then once more he patted John's knee. "There's something I want to tell you . . . before you go tomorrow."

John slid his arm around Zechariah's waist. "I love when we have these talks." Their eyes met. "I'll miss this most of all."

"Yes." Zechariah took a deep breath, blinking back the tears he couldn't yet shed. "Son, where you are going you will learn in silence. That's what the desert is for — so that when you're not learning the Torah, you can be quiet before the Lord."

"The way you were, Dad? Before I was born?" John peered up at him, clearly seeing the connection.

"Yes. The way I was." Zechariah thought back to those days when he couldn't speak. "God used the days of silence. He put a song in my heart but I couldn't sing it until the right time." Zechariah smiled at his boy. "The right time was the moment we named you John. Then I could speak, and the first thing I did was praise God with the song."

John was quiet for a few minutes. He threw another stone into the stream. "Dad." Their eyes met again. "I think God will put a song in my heart, too. While I'm in the desert."

"Really?" Zechariah felt his heart breaking, felt the loss of this precious boy as he would feel it every day of his life after John left. "You're probably right. And when the time comes, if the Lord gives you a song, He will give you the chance to sing it."

John nodded, thoughtful. He stared at the water once more. "Thanks for talking to me."

"I love you, son. Being your father . . . it has been the greatest joy in my life."

Before they left their favorite spot, Zechariah put his hand on John's shoulder. "I want to bless you, son."

"Thank you." John grinned again. "I'm going to need it."

Zechariah closed his eyes. "Father, prepare him for his role in the salvation of Your people. Please, Father, protect him. No matter how difficult things become in the years ahead, help him remember this moment. And how very much he is loved."

"Amen." John stood.

"God be with you, my son. I will hold you in my heart every day you're away."

"This will always be my home, Father."

With that, twelve years were behind them and in the morning John was gone. Tears spilled from Zechariah's eyes as he watched his boy leave, and this time he didn't try to stop them. Zechariah did not know the exact plans for John. He did not know where God would take him once his training was complete, or when. He also didn't know what he'd done to deserve such a wonderful son.

But he knew this: every day that passed he would be thankful to God for the years they'd had with John. And something else.

He would miss his boy as long as he lived.

STORY 3
JOHN THE BAPTIST
THE CHOSEN COUSIN

John took a final look back at his home, and at his parents standing in the doorway. His mom was wiping her tears. John waved, and for a moment he wished he could turn around and run back. Pretend he was still eleven and life between him and them would go on the way it always had.

His parents waved in return, and his father kept his hand high in the air. *It's a sign,* John thought. As if his father was reminding him of his promise. *We'll be here waiting whenever you come home.*

"Bye," he whispered. He walked backward a few steps. "For now."

The road was turning, and so John had no choice. He tried to memorize the way his parents looked, standing in front of the only home he'd ever known. Then he turned around and faced the road ahead.

"It'll be okay." His teacher glanced at him. "Leaving is always hard at first."

John nodded and stuck his chin out. He didn't want to cry. His leaving was the right thing — he could sense that deep in his soul. John had always been set apart from other kids. He could *feel* things. Right and wrong things. When something was right, it resonated inside him. No other kids had that.

Except Jesus.

"You okay?" The rabbi looked at him, his brow raised.

"Yes, sir. I'm fine now."

A knowing filled John. This whole journey was about Jesus, about preparing people for Jesus. Telling them about Him. His cousin, his best friend. The pieces didn't quite fit together yet. But they would one day soon. And when they did, John knew this much for sure: Jesus would be at the center of it all.

It was time to go home, time for his regular visit, and John could hardly wait. Ten years had passed in a rich and beautiful mix of studying the Torah and listening to God. John was twenty-two now, and his purpose had never been more pressing in his heart. His time at the school had been well spent: learning every day, but listening, too. So much listening. Sometimes he would spend days in the desert by himself, just sitting in silence, sleeping on the sandy ground under the stars, pondering the mystery of God's love for His people.

Still, John loved the fact that twice a year he got to go home.

His pack held a flask of water and some basic food. John's diet had changed since he'd been training for God. He could survive on very little now — whatever he could harvest from the desert floor. Locusts, mostly. And honey from the comb. John had learned how to work around the desert bees and take in enough sustenance.

"See you in a week." John nodded to the rabbi.

"Look for God in the journey." His teacher's eyes narrowed, full of wisdom. "Even when you are away from school, the Father is teaching. Be listening."

John hesitated, taking the matter seriously. "Always."

His parents were older now. Old enough that every visit made John wonder if it might be his last. He was thankful they were healthy, but the truth about their age drove home what the rabbi had told him. He must pay attention. God would no doubt have something for him on this visit.

Before he reached the door, his father

stepped outside. He held up his hand — the same way he had when John left home the first time. His welcoming, encouraging, loving father. Even still, the man's smile lit up the sometimes lonely places in John's heart.

He jogged the rest of the distance and like that, he was in his dad's arms. "Dad . . . I've missed you."

His father kissed his head. "Me, too, son."

"John! You're home!" His mother met them in the doorway and John hugged her next.

"Mom!" John kissed her cheek and then grinned at his father. "It's been too long."

"You look older." She brushed John's hair off his forehead. "But still so handsome."

John laughed. "I feel older." His smile faded some as he caught his father's eye. "My time is coming. God makes the journey ahead clearer all the time."

In the days that followed, John cherished every hour with his parents. His mother needed more help than before. But since his calling was far out in the desert, his parents had to rely on other people to help them. One afternoon John watched a neighbor girl stop by to check on his mother's garden.

"Who is she?" John peered out the door

of the house at the patch of vegetables beyond. "She's pretty."

His mother smiled. "That's Anne. She lives down the street. The two of you used to play together."

"That's Anne?" John looked at his mother, then back at the girl helping outside. "She's beautiful."

"Yes." His mother raised an eyebrow in his direction, but just as quickly she returned to her baking. "Her husband died shortly after they were married. That was several years ago." She paused. "You should tell her hello."

"I will." John didn't hesitate. His time in the desert was perfect for his soul. But a conversation with a girl his age was impossible.

Until now.

He tucked his curly hair behind his ears and straightened his shoulders. Anne was collecting vegetables in a woven basket, and as he drew closer he could hear her singing. A song Jewish kids learned when they were young, music to one of the Psalms. John stopped and watched her, taken by her. Then he closed the distance between them. "Anne. Hello."

She caught her breath as she turned around. "My goodness, John." Her eyes shone in the late afternoon sun. "You scared me."

"I'm sorry." He chuckled and took a step closer. "My mom says you've been helping her." His eyes took in the sight of the well-kept garden. "I wanted to thank you."

"Your father does so much for the people of the town." She smiled. "It's the least I can do." Her hesitation seemed intentional. "As long as you're gone, anyway."

"Well . . . thank you." John wanted to make the conversation last longer. "Your help . . . it means a lot."

Anne stood and dusted the dirt off her hands. Her hair fell to her waist. "How long are you home?"

The cost of his calling rarely hit John. But this was one of those times. "Just this week." He drew a long breath. "Then I go back."

"To the desert? Is that where you've been, John?" Anne brushed her hair back from her face. "Studying the Scriptures?"

"Yes." John couldn't take his eyes off her. He could hardly think in her presence. "I'm . . . preparing for my calling. I'm home only a couple times a year."

A shadow fell over her face. "That's what your mother said." She nodded. "When will you be home for good?"

John thought for a moment. "Whenever

I've completed the task God has for me." He didn't want to explain his role in preparing the way for the Messiah. "God is speaking to me in the desert. When it's time, He'll let me know."

"Whenever that is . . . when you're finished with that task . . . then will you come home?"

Again John let her words run through his heart. "Yes." He felt a ripple of joy start inside and make its way to his face. "Yes, when I've finished the work God has for me, I'll come home."

"Well." Anne's smile came easily, as genuine as the summer breeze. "I'll look forward to that day, then."

John didn't remember feeling the ground as he headed into the house. His mother was watching him. "You looked very happy out there."

"She's wonderful." He allowed a nervous laugh. "I can't believe that's little Anne. All grown up." Again the cost weighed heavily on John's heart. "Her husband had no brothers?"

"No." His mom sighed and when her eyes met his, he saw a deeper understanding. "Since her husband died, I think she's waiting. For a time when . . ."

"When what?"

His mother reached for his hand. "When you come home again."

As the evening settled over them, John pondered his time with Anne, his talk with his mother. His father found him out back by the stream, watching the stars.

"I thought you'd be here." His dad came up beside him and leaned on the same rock. "You always loved the water."

"Yes."

His father put his arm around his shoulders. For a long while they were quiet. "Your being called by God . . . I knew it would never be easy. Not for any of us."

John hesitated. "It won't be too much longer."

"You'll be ready. Whenever the time comes."

That night after they'd gone into the house, John thought about the future. If he managed to finish his work for God and still make it home in the next few years, and if Anne was still living down the street . . .

He let the thought fall away. His heart and mind and soul were completely dedicated to God. To Him. His mission first.

Whatever happened after that would have to wait.

The calling came a month after John's

thirtieth birthday.

He was studying in the desert, memorizing Scripture, and waiting on the Lord when he heard the voice. John wasn't sure if he heard it in his heart or if the voice boomed across the barren desert floor. But the message was clear: John needed to go to the countryside around the Jordan River and baptize people, burying them in water and raising them up out of it to a new life, a new understanding of God.

John listened intently. Baptism would symbolize a death to the old ways, and the promise of new life for those who turned away from sin. Because the sins of the people were rampant and widespread, it would be John's job to warn them of the dangers of evil and urge them to turn to God instead. And he would do so waist-deep in the Jordan River. John pictured the stream behind his parents' house and he could only smile. He had always known water would be involved.

The scope and breadth of the task ahead felt daunting, but John was ready. He was tough from nearly two decades of living in the desert, eating locusts and honey, and he felt up to the job God had for him. The Holy Spirit was with him — John felt that more keenly than ever.

He sent a message to his parents. "My time has come," the message read. "I'm being called to the land around the River Jordan. I will baptize people there, and prepare them for the coming Messiah. I feel ready and excited about what lays ahead. Pray for me." He finished the letter with words that were truer than time. "I'm going to sing my song, Dad. I love you and Mom always. Your son, John."

He set out the next morning, and along the way God pressed upon his heart a Scripture from Isaiah. *A messenger is calling out in the desert, "Prepare the way for the Lord. Make straight paths for Him. Every valley will be filled in. Every mountain and hill will be made level. The crooked roads will become straight. The rough ways will become smooth. And everyone will see God's salvation."*

Suddenly in a burst of clarity John understood. The prophet that Isaiah had been talking about was John himself! Zechariah and Elizabeth's only son — of all people. He wasn't just preparing the way for the people near the Jordan River. According to the prophet, he would prepare the way for all people. Everywhere.

The realization was more than John could take in, and it propelled him to the Jordan River in what felt like no time. As John neared the water, he remembered a thousand times when he'd sat behind his home, tossing pebbles into the stream. Pondering right and wrong.

In a loud voice, John called to the people who passed by. As he did, God gave him stern words, harsh accusations. John felt righteous anger in his soul, as if God was allowing him to feel the sins of the people personally. "You are like a nest of poisonous snakes!" he cried out. "Who warned you to escape the coming of God's anger?"

A few people came to listen, and then a few more.

John stood steady in his sandals and desert clothes made from camel's hair. Attached to his leather belt was a sack of locusts and wild honey. All he needed. He raised his voice again. "Produce fruit that shows you have turned away from your sins."

Soon a crowd had gathered, many from Jerusalem and Judea. Some of them wanted to know how to repent, how to turn away from their sins. "Be baptized!" John called out. And so the people came to be baptized. John would plunge them beneath the water — dead to their old lives. As they came up out of the water, he would declare them clean, ready to live new lives for God.

But some stood along the shore and complained about John. "Our father is Abraham. That man can't tell us what to do," one of them said.

John heard the criticism. He spun around and stared. "Don't start saying to yourselves, 'Abraham is our father.' " He set his sandaled foot on a pile of rocks. "Your lineage won't save you now. I tell you, God can raise up children for Abraham even from these stones."

The crowd grew silent and John pointed at the naysayers. He warned them of God's wrath.

At that, the crowd looked genuinely frightened. They yelled at once, "Then what should we do?"

John took a few steps closer. "If you have extra clothes, you should share with those who have none. And if you have extra food, you should do the same."

The people were amazed, and many lined up to be baptized in the Jordan River. A few days passed, and still more people came. Among them were tax collectors looking to be baptized. As they drew near the water, they called out, "Teacher, what should we do?"

John felt compassion toward them, but he knew their sins because God had shown him. "Don't collect any more than you are required to."

Soldiers came next. "And what should we do?"

Again John knew their hearts. "Don't force people to give you money. Don't bring false charges against people." He looked straight through them, to their hearts. "Be happy with your pay."

The crowds grew larger. After hundreds of years of silence, they wondered if John might be the Christ.

When he got word of this, he held up his hands and waited until he had the attention of the crowd. "I baptize you with water. But One who is more powerful than I am will come." He looked at the faces gathered at the river. "I'm not good enough to untie the straps of His sandals. He will baptize you with the Holy Spirit and with fire. His pitchfork is in His hand to toss the straw away from the threshing floor."

The people moved in closer, gripped by John's words.

"He will gather the wheat into His storeroom. But He will burn up the husks with fire that can't be put out."

The people understood he was talking about them. They needed to repent of their sins — they needed forgiveness, or they would be cut off from God. And so people came by the hundreds so John could baptize them.

Every night when he finally crawled into his tent, John could feel just one thing: pure and complete joy. He thought about his dad's experience with silence, and the music that had built inside him. After so many years of silence in the desert, this wasn't only his calling, the one his father had always told him was coming.

It was his song.

The longer John stayed in the countryside near the Jordan River, the more two things became very clear: First, Jesus had left His home and started His ministry, because people were talking about Him. Second, John knew now that the current King Herod, ruler of Galilee, had a deep sin problem. Herod was living with his brother's wife — a woman named Herodias. That was only the beginning of Herod's many sins against God. The Holy Spirit had made it clear to John, and he began to call out the king.

When Herod would pass by with his entourage, John would shout truths at him: "You must repent, King Herod! You have sinned against God many times in many ways. And now you have your brother's wife as your own." He pointed as King Herod ordered his procession to continue on. "Wait! You are at risk of being cut down even as you go about your duties! You must repent if you are to be right with God! Turn away from your sins! The kingdom of heaven is near."

One day after Herod had passed by, a commotion came from just over the nearest hill. John turned that way and there coming up over the grassy knoll was his best friend. His cousin.

His Savior.

As soon as Jesus's face came into view, their eyes met and both men froze. How many hours had they played together as boys, and how long had God been preparing them for what was ahead? Now, in this moment, it was as if no time had passed.

But something had changed. The man coming toward him was not only his family member. He was God in the flesh. The reality took John's breath and made him steady his legs to keep from falling to his knees.

Jesus smiled and made His way to John. His followers came with Him, and when they reached the edge of the water they stopped. Jesus took a few steps into the Jordan River. "Hello, John."

"Jesus . . . You've come."

"Yes." The warmth in Jesus's eyes was the same as it had been when He was a boy. "I want you to baptize Me."

John shook his head, not understanding. "I need to be baptized by *You.* So why do You come to me?"

Jesus put His hand on John's shoulder. "Let it be this way for now. It is right for us to do this." He looked over His shoulder at the massive crowd, curious, watching. Then Jesus turned back to John. "This carries out God's holy plan."

In a rush, a dawning of light flooded John's heart and he understood. John had to prepare the people for Jesus. But Jesus wanted to be baptized to show the people what living a life for God looked like. Baptism represented a death to the old way of life. Jesus was leaving His former life and starting His ministry. His example would be for all people, for all time.

Baptism was part of the beginning.

"Okay, then." John held out his hands and helped Jesus over the rocks to where the Jordan River was a little deeper. Then beneath the watchful looks of countless people from Jerusalem and Judea and many neighboring villages, John lowered Jesus into the water and raised Him back up again.

As soon as Jesus came out of the water, something happened that no one had ever seen. Not even John. Heaven opened up — cracked right open — and something like a dove flew down and landed on Jesus's shoulder. At the same time a booming voice from heaven said, "This is My Son, and I love Him. I am very pleased with Him."

All around them people cried out. Some fell to their knees.

"What miracle is this?" several of them shouted. "Father, have mercy on us!"

Only Jesus didn't look shocked.

The voice faded, and heaven closed, returning to sky — the way it had looked before Jesus's baptism. With that, Jesus turned to John. The look in His eyes said it all. This might be good-bye for a long time. John found his voice. "I will pray for You every day." His gaze didn't waver. "And I'll keep telling people the truth about their sin, about repenting so they might find You."

They shared a smile and then they hugged for a long time. The hug of two best friends, ready for another separation.

And whatever came with it.

Jesus had been gone a few months when Herod came back. By then, several of John's followers had left to follow Jesus. John was glad. He wished everyone would follow Jesus instead of him. That was the point. Besides, Roman politics and Jewish customs and traditions were constantly coming into conflict. The Jewish people wanted a king and there was talk that Jesus might be the One they were waiting for. Herod was worried about that and frustrated with John's declarations against him.

This time Herod came with a larger entourage, including Herodias — his brother's wife. Like every day since John began teaching, crowds of people stood along the banks of the Jordan, listening to John and waiting to be baptized. But the crowd fell silent as King Herod drew near.

By then a tension had developed between Herod and John, and most of the people who came to be baptized knew about it.

"King Herod, have you come to repent of your evil ways?" John called out. He wasn't afraid of the king. God had chosen him to help people repent instead of give their lives to sin. Herod was no exception.

"Listen here, John the Baptist." The king motioned for his driver to stop. Herod looked at Herodias and then back at John. "How dare you call me out in front of the crowd?"

"I do what God tells me to do." John stood straight. He would not back down. King Herod was merely a man. John's years of training in the desert had readied him for this moment. "You are sleeping with your brother's wife." He turned his stare to Herodias. "You both know you're doing wrong. God is calling you to repent, King Herod. The ax is already at the base of the tree. All trees that don't produce good fruit will be cut down."

Herod's face grew dark red. His followers stared at him and then at John, clearly anxious to see who would win this battle. Herodias turned to Herod and said something none of them could hear. Suddenly Herod raised his voice. "John the Baptist, you have taken this too far. You will not demean the king of Galilee!" He looked at his soldiers. "Arrest him! Now!"

Not for a moment did John actually think he would be arrested. God was with him, His Spirit was in him. This was his calling since before birth. But even as John thought these things, Herod's soldiers strode toward him.

"What's happening?" one of the people nearby cried out. "You can't arrest John the Baptizer! We need him!"

John looked to the water, the place where

he had met with countless souls looking to turn their lives over to God. The water that had drawn him since he was a young boy. *God, whatever attack this is, I can handle it. Give me strength and show me the way out.*

The soldiers were closing the distance. "Don't move!" one of them yelled. Their swords were drawn and as they came closer, the crowd shrank back.

Fear breathed, hot and unfamiliar, against the back of John's neck. He stuck out his chest. He wouldn't be afraid. "I am God's messenger! Produce fruit that shows you have turned away from your sins!" He pointed at King Herod. "Yes, Herod. That goes for even you. Turn from your sins!"

Herodias touched the king's hand.

"Hurry up!" Herod shouted. "Arrest him!"

The soldiers reached John, and in that second everything spun wildly out of control. One of the soldiers shoved him while another two grabbed his wrists and bound them with chains. The world around him began to tilt. What was happening? Why was God allowing this? "Father! I am Your servant!" John cried out. But even as he spoke, the first soldier pushed him to his knees.

"You can do your preaching in prison!"

the soldier spat at him.

This had to be God's plan. They would take him to prison and Herod and his court would all change their ways. Okay, fine. But John wasn't going without a fight. He was about to stand up when a pair of soldiers began dragging him through the dirt, over rocks and brush. John was stronger than they knew. He jerked back, stopping the soldiers long enough to struggle to his feet.

After that, John refused to go down again. They shoved him. The soldiers in front pulled him, repeatedly trying to drop him to his knees. But John wouldn't fall. Whatever was happening to him, this was temporary.

They slammed him into a wagon and took him to a prison near Herod's palace. The whole way there people stopped and stared at him. "I will return! Repent and be baptized!" he called out. "The kingdom of heaven is near."

When he passed by they shouted, "There he is! John the Baptizer!"

When they reached the prison, John was thrown into a dank underground cell no bigger than his parents' kitchen. The guards took the chains off his wrists and slammed the bars shut. As they locked it John raised his voice. "You've been tricked into working for a snake." He gave the bars a single shake as the guards walked away. "Repent and turn from your sins!"

"Yeah, yeah," one of the guards looked over his shoulder and yelled back at him. Then with the slam of another door, John was alone.

His sides heaved from the effort of fighting against the guards. John backed up slowly against the far wall. *That's fine,* he thought. They could lock him up for now. He was God's messenger. Someone would get him out of here, and then he'd get back to baptizing at the Jordan.

It was only a matter of time.

John wasn't alone. He knew that. The Holy Spirit still lived in him, comforting and reminding him of the Scriptures he'd studied since he was a boy. Patience had always been a deep well for John, something he'd learned in the desert. Something that came with the presence of God.

But this was different.

God had called him to baptize at the Jordan River, he was certain. Only now he was in the middle of his mission, and somehow he'd been thrown into prison. There were still so many people to share the good news with, so many to baptize, especially since

Jesus's ministry was well under way. Word had reached John a few weeks before his arrest that Jesus had survived a testing time in the desert and now He was telling people about the kingdom of God and performing miracles. Everyone was talking about Him.

John walked across his darkened prison cell and gripped the bars. But what about him? He and Jesus were supposed to work together. They had been born at the same time and visited each other every Passover. And now when the time had finally come to prepare the way, to tell the world the truth about Jesus and salvation, John was stuck in this wretched hole.

"Let me out!" he shouted into the darkness. He rattled the bars again. "You can't keep me here!"

He waited but there was no response, no laughter from the guards, no hint of a conversation. Then after a few minutes he heard the sound of doors opening and gruff voices. John listened, familiar with the sound. They were bringing in another prisoner.

Many had occupied the cells on either side of him since his arrival. Most were in such bad shape from the soldiers' handling they couldn't talk. Only one had known who John was. None of them knew what Herod planned to do with him. John peered down the hallway. Maybe this man would know more.

The guards held a lantern and even though the light hurt John's eyes it felt wonderful. A few distant rays of daylight shone into the hallway every day for an hour or so. But it wasn't enough to see by. John squinted, watching the scene play out before him. The guards were rougher with this prisoner, whatever he'd done wrong. They shoved him into the cell across from John and when his body crumpled to the floor they laughed.

"Get me out of here!" John yelled at them. "I've done nothing wrong!"

"Silence!" One of the guards came up close to the bars and glared at John. "You've offended King Herod. You're not going anywhere." The guard turned and walked off.

"I am a messenger for God!" John shouted. "He will hold you accountable for this! You and all the guards!"

The man was gone. John's heart pounded in his chest. God would have a special punishment for Herod and his men, no doubt. He peered through his bars at the man in the cell opposite his. "Hello." He waited. "Can you hear me?"

A desperate moan came from the man. "I must . . . still be alive. I can hear you."

"What did you do, man?" John felt compassion for him, whatever his offense. "Why are you here?"

"T . . . treason." The man's words came slowly and with great effort. "I spoke out . . . against King Herod." He coughed a few times. "You?"

"I am John the Baptizer." John waited. "Have you heard of me?"

"Yes. I know you." The man seemed more emotional. He took a few quick breaths and his voice cracked. "You baptized me. In the Jordan River."

The news hit John at the center of his heart. "You have repented of your sins?"

"Yes." The man was crying now, sobs wracking his body. "I want . . . to live for God."

John felt a smile tug at his lips for the first time since they'd thrown him in prison. "And so you will, man. You will live for Him."

"They . . . said they would kill me!" Fear was clearly strangling him.

"God's kingdom is not of this world, my friend." John peered through the darkness, barely making out the shape of the prisoner. The man had struggled to his feet, despite his obvious pain. John forced himself to sound calm. "This earth is not our home. Whatever happens, God is in control. He wants you to —"

From the far side of the hall the gates rattled again and they heard the voices of the guards. The peace of God rose within John, a peace that had been his closest companion in the desert all those years. "You belong to God now," John spoke louder than before. "He will never leave you."

"Silence, John the Baptizer." One of the guards clanked his sword against the bars of John's cell. "Your time is coming."

The guard turned to the cell across from John's. "Your time, however, is right now."

"No!" the prisoner cried out. "I'm innocent."

"God is with you!" John yelled louder than the guards. "Remember your decision at the Jordan River."

"Silence!" A different guard kicked the bars of John's cell.

"Feel God's peace, man." John wouldn't stop preaching. This was what he was born for. Let them kill him if that's what they were going to do. He raised his voice again. "God is with you! He will bring you home!"

But even while John was yelling truth to

the prisoner, the guards opened the man's cell door and in a single swift movement, one of them drove a sword through his chest.

"There." The nearest guard snarled at him. "Now you have no one to preach at." He laughed out loud. "Herod wanted us to kill him here where you could watch. So you'd know what's ahead for you."

John shoved his hands at the bars, rocking the door with a sudden jolt. "You have a choice, men. Repent so you won't be thrown into the fires!" John yelled with everything in him. He pointed at the dead body in the shadows of the other cell. "Go to your eternal home, man. Go in peace!"

Righteous sorrow shook John's body head to foot, and he stared at the guards as they grabbed the man's limp hands and feet. Each word came out with deliberate force. "That . . . man . . . is with God."

The guards only laughed and dragged the body away, and once again John was by himself. Alone with the Holy Spirit. Most executions were done in the public eye — a way of keeping the people in line. But this man had been killed here in the prison clearly as a way of intimidating John. At Herod's request.

He closed his eyes. Now one of his followers was dead.

Dead for being part of this new movement, repentance from sins and turning back to God. Dead for publicly disclaiming Herod. John blinked a few times in the darkness and then slowly he slid against the wall to the floor. If that's how Herod's men treated that man, then how would they treat John, when his time came?

He shuddered, and a chill ran down his spine. He needed to talk to Jesus.

His cousin was the Savior, God in the flesh. John understood that perfectly. But then why did it seem like everything was falling apart? All his life he had prepared for this job, trained for the purpose of telling people about the coming Messiah. So then the crowds should still be headed to the Jordan River, and John should still be there baptizing, right?

He looked at the empty cell across from him. The dead prisoner should be home, telling other people in his village about repentance and the gift of God's forgiveness. John felt sick to his stomach. Things would be easier if he could just understand, if he could see order in the chaos, a script playing out.

If only he could talk to Jesus.

■ ■ ■ ■

Dark days followed for John. Prisoners came and left. Some were killed. Some knew about the movement at the Jordan River and about Jesus. Others hadn't heard of it. With each passing day John felt his enthusiasm grow dim.

Yes, he still felt the presence of the Spirit. But his purpose no longer felt certain. What if he hadn't heard the Lord correctly? What if he should have waited another year before heading to the Jordan River? Maybe he'd been too anxious, too overzealous. By the time John heard the calling, he was full of a holy sort of anger at the sins of the people. He could hardly wait to show them the error of their ways and turn them back to God again.

Maybe his approach had been wrong.

Questions pelted him like so many rocks in a windstorm of doubt. Maybe God was punishing him for leaving the desert too soon. He should've gone home and talked about the calling with his father. Surely his dad would've known what to do. Instead John had hurried off at the first sign of God's leading.

What he thought was God's leading.

The damp walls and rancid smells were beginning to suffocate him. Rotted human remains and putrid waste. The guards fed him just once a day, and now he could feel his bones poking through his skin. Darkness closed in like a lion. John tried to stay strong in the storm of questions, but he was losing the battle. This couldn't be God's will, that he waste away here in prison.

John paced his cell, grabbing at his unruly hair, desperate for a way out. Then the most awful question of all seized his heart and soul. What if . . . what if Jesus wasn't the Messiah? What if John was supposed to wait for someone else? His anger and doubt swirled together and came out as a cry in the darkness. "God, where are You?"

The moment he finished the question, the gates at the end of the hallway opened. It wasn't the usual sharp sound John had become accustomed to. He moved quietly to the edge of his cell and grabbed hold of the bars.

"Who's there?"

"John?" the man whispered his name. He carried a lantern and moved closer. "John the Baptizer?"

"Yes." This was not the voice of one of the regular guards. John stayed still, waiting.

"John, I am one of your disciples." The

man came to the edge of John's cell. "Here." He handed over a piece of bread. "Eat."

This was not the desert, and his locusts and honey had long since run out. John took the bread and stuffed it into his mouth, ravenous after days of starving. "Thank you, friend." His words were muffled as he ate. "How did you find me?"

"This week I was promoted to guard. I'm on official business." The man looked over his shoulder back at the gate. No one was in sight. "I'm supposed to be checking on you for Herod."

"When is he going to let me out?" The bread was gone, and John's stomach growled for more.

"Listen." The man kept to a whisper. "I have news for you."

John waited, amazed. He had asked for help and now God had sent it. "Go on. Please."

"Herod doesn't want to harm you." The man checked over his shoulder again. "It's Herodias. She has it out for you, John. She hates that you proclaimed her sins in front of the people. She wants you killed, but Herod won't allow it because he knows you're a holy man." The guard spoke quickly, anxious to deliver his message. "Herod used to pass by the Jordan River just to hear you preach."

"Then why didn't he repent?" This was the first news John had heard since he was locked up. Hope lifted his heart.

"You puzzled him, but Herodias hated everything you said." The man wiped a layer of sweat off his forehead. "I have to hurry."

"Continue. Please."

"That's all, really."

"What about Jesus of Nazareth?" John's heart pounded so loud he could hear it. "What do you know about Him?"

The man shrugged. "People are talking. He is teaching and preaching in the towns of Galilee."

John nodded, and his eyes drifted to the uneven rocky floor of his cell. That was all? Jesus was teaching and preaching? While John sat in this prison cell?

"I have to leave." The man's eyes met John's. "How can I serve you? What do you need?"

"I have a single request." John heard the brokenness in his own voice. "Find Jesus. Ask Him if He is the One who is supposed to come . . . or should we look for someone else?"

The man reached through the bars and squeezed John's hand. "I'll do it. I'll find the answer."

"Thank you."

John watched him leave. Of all the waiting he'd done since leaving home when he was twelve years old, the time ahead would be the longest. What if Jesus wasn't the Messiah? What if John was supposed to prepare the way for another man? How awful would that be? He felt sick to his stomach.

It would be more awful than anything John could imagine.

In the days that followed, John forced himself to eat and drink. He needed his strength, needed to be alert and ready for action whenever the answer came about Jesus. But so he wouldn't go crazy waiting, trapped in darkness and horrible smells, John did the only thing he could do.

He traveled back in time.

His life had been a series of studying Scripture and waiting in silence, punctuated by some of the happiest, brightest moments a man could have. Usually he would start at the beginning, back when he was still a boy. If he thought about it long enough, the air around him would clear and he could feel himself taking in the sweet breeze from behind his parents' house.

He closed his eyes and he was there again. Catching a rabbit with his father and setting him in a basket for his mother to see. And he was running into the house, about to show her when the little critter jumped out and began hopping around the room. His mother was screaming and he and his father were laughing.

And he was eight and nine and ten and he and his parents were welcoming Jesus and His family at the Passover and he and Jesus were running down the street, racing and gathering all the kids in the village to play together. He could see Jesus's eyes. The kindest, most sincere eyes anyone could ever have. His cousin, his best friend.

John breathed in deep. The smell of warm bread filled his senses and he was in the kitchen again, eleven years old, watching his mother bake. And she was telling him that he had to be careful with the yeast. A little yeast would work its way through the whole loaf of bread. And they were laughing and talking and then he was older.

Twenty-two and home for a visit.

And his mother was looking out the door at the neighbor, Anne, helping in the garden. The beautiful girl with the long hair. And she was turning around and smiling at him. A smile he had never forgotten. And she was saying, "When will you be home for good?"

And John was trying to find the words, but the only words he could say were these: "Whenever I've completed the task God has for me." The words played in his mind again. *Whenever I complete the task. Whenever that is.*

And he was realizing that if his life had been different, Anne might have been his wife and they might've had a family. Children to call his own. His mom would've been a wonderful grandmother. If Anne had been his . . .

He stopped the memory there, on the sweet face of Anne, the girl he had played with as a child.

Then he could feel the desert sand between his toes as he made the trek once more to his school, feel the sun on his shoulders. One Scripture after another passed through his mind like a most magnificent tapestry. God's Word in him, through him, around him.

John was still replaying all the things good and true about his life when he heard the rattling of the gate. A soft sound like the time before — when his follower had come to talk to him. John opened his eyes and stood. "Who is it?"

The guard carried a lantern and walked quickly to his cell. "It is me," he whispered.

"Your friend." Once more he handed John a piece of bread — larger than before. "For you."

"Thank you." John took a quick bite, but his eyes stayed on the guard. "You've met with Jesus?"

"Yes." He looked at John a long time. "I have your answer."

John wasn't sure what to feel. Sweat broke out across his forehead and his mouth went dry. The pounding of his heart filled his ears. His whole life had led to this moment. John struggled to catch his breath. His memories couldn't help him now. He had to be in the moment. Whatever the news. "You asked Him . . . the question?"

"I did. I asked if He was the One." The man reached through the bars and grabbed hold of John's hand. "Jesus told me to tell you this: 'The blind can see. The deaf can hear. The broken walk. Those with leprosy are healed.'" The man's voice cracked. "And the dead are raised to life."

For the first time since he was twelve years old, John could do nothing to stop the tears. They built up in the dry desert of his broken heart and spilled down his thin face. "He . . . said those things?"

"Yes, John." The man withdrew his hand and paced a few steps. "He told me to tell you all of that." He stopped and looked at John. "Everyone's talking about Him. Jesus is the Messiah. I have no doubt whatsoever."

John nodded. "Okay, then. If Jesus said that, so be it."

"He told me to tell you blessed are those who do not give up their faith because of Him."

John pictured Jesus, coming down the hill to the Jordan River, and the Spirit of God lighting on Him like a dove. He rubbed his fists across his cheeks, trying to stop the tears. "He . . . said that?"

"He did." The guard was back at the bars of John's cell. "As I was leaving, I heard Jesus talking to the crowd about you. So I stopped and listened. You should know what He said."

John held on to every word. He had missed so much living in this prison cell. Now he could almost see his cousin preaching to the people, almost hear His voice calling out loud. The voice of the Savior. "Please go on."

The man nodded. "Jesus told them no one better than John the Baptist had ever been born. But even then, the least person in the kingdom of heaven is greater than you, John. Heaven is more important."

John's tears came again.

Jesus cared about him. He hadn't forgotten His cousin sitting in a prison cell. The comfort John gleaned from those words made him feel as if Jesus had stepped into the dank cell and hugged him the way He had at the Jordan River. Jesus was the Messiah. John had played his part and prepared the way, whatever happened from this point on.

"You look different." The guard leaned in closer. "Are you okay?"

"I'm perfect." John wiped his tears again. "That's what I needed to hear." He reached through the bars. "Thank you, my friend."

"Of course." He looked over his shoulder. "I'll try to keep you posted. The king is having a big dinner now for his birthday. Herodias's daughter is dancing for the king." The man shook his head. "I don't think God would be pleased with any of it."

There was a rattling at the gate, and the guard jumped. "I have to go. I'll pray for you."

"Thanks." John raised his hand and held it up as the man hurried off. But as the guard left, three others walked into the prison. They were laughing and talking much louder than John's friend.

"I knew it would happen this way," one of

them said. "Herodias gets whatever she wants."

"It was the girl, not the mother." A second guard laughed. Then he switched to a mocking voice. "Whatever you want . . . up to half the kingdom."

"It's a fitting gift for her mother, that's for sure." The first guard joined in the laughter. "John the Baptist's head on a platter."

John reeled backward, back to the corner of his cell. His head on a platter? They were going to kill him? Because that's what Herodias's daughter wanted? He stayed there, unmoving as they reached his cell.

"Time's up, John the Baptist!" The three of them laughed, much louder than before. "No more preaching for you!"

More words came from their mouths, but John could no longer hear them. The sounds and smells changed, and he could feel the sun on his shoulders. He remembered the Scriptures, the promises of God. A joyful life lay just ahead. The least in the kingdom of heaven would be greater than anyone on earth. John smiled.

He could hardly wait.

The men were moving closer, and one of them pulled out a sword. They dragged him out of the cell and down the hallway. John kept his eyes closed, but he knew it was coming, knew what was about to happen.

Peace ran through his veins, his heartbeat and breathing slow and steady. He could smell the bread and hear his mother's voice. "Be careful to use the right amount of yeast, John." And his father was sitting next to him at the stream and John could feel the summer breeze against his skin. And he was chasing a baby rabbit, calling to his father to bring the basket, and then carrying the critter into the house to show his mother and . . .

There was a flash of light and in a single heartbeat the darkness was gone and there was nothing but light.

The most beautiful light John had ever seen.

Story 4
Elizabeth
THE FAITHFUL AUNT

Elizabeth tried to hold out hope.

John had been in prison for a year now. A long, painful year of missing her son and being unsure of his condition, and wanting nothing more than to hold him in her arms again. That was the hardest part, the not knowing — whether he was being tortured or taken care of, whether he was struggling with his calling.

The way Elizabeth struggled on some days.

She and Zechariah thought often about taking the trip to Galilee and begging King Herod's guards for a visit. Just one chance to see John face-to-face. But they were too old for the journey. Zechariah's legs weren't strong and Elizabeth had trouble breathing. Otherwise nothing would've stopped them from getting to him. Besides, John couldn't have visitors. That's what people in the town had heard. He was in one of the worst cells in all of Herod's kingdom.

Elizabeth stood at the doorway of her home and looked up. Clouds covered the afternoon sky. Days like this she missed John even more. Mostly because she and Zechariah still lived and worked and slept in the same house where they had raised their son. His little-boy memories were woven into every stone that made up the place.

Elizabeth returned to the basin in the kitchen. The olives still needed pressing. She began working on them, the way she'd done a thousand times. God had blessed them with old age — a gift many couples didn't get. But at this point, heaven wasn't far off for either of them. Elizabeth wanted only to live long enough to see John again, to see him freed from the prison cell.

To that end, she prayed constantly.

She exhaled softly, washed her hands in the basin, and dried them. The smell of fresh baked bread filled the kitchen. That was about all she could accomplish in a day anymore. Baking the bread, pressing the olive oil, and praying for John. Always that. A simple life, but one full of happy memories and sweet moments with Zechariah.

And there was Anne.

Elizabeth believed with all her heart that

Anne was waiting, hoping, that one day John would be set free and — having fulfilled his calling — come home again. A smile filled Elizabeth's heart. That would be something. To live long enough to see John come home, to see if her only child might find love this late in her life. She breathed in deeply, comforted by the possibilities. The bread needed covering, so she put a cloth over it and returned to her spot near the door.

A patch of blue sky had opened overhead. Elizabeth smiled.

God had not forgotten them. He was here, now, and He was with John — even in a terrible prison cell. One day their son would be released and — no matter how far off — she and Zechariah would see him again. Her skirt blew around her ankles in the breeze, the cool air gentle against her cheeks.

What was John doing right now? How was life in his prison cell? *God, let him feel Your presence —*

Wailing stopped Elizabeth's prayer mid-sentence. A group of men and women were heading up the road toward her. The women in the group were crying out to God. Elizabeth's heart slammed around in her chest. What was this? What had happened? Zechariah was usually home by now — had he

146

fallen, or . . . ?

Elizabeth couldn't finish her thought. The group was coming closer, and other people from the village were joining in. She took a few shaky steps out the front door and then she heard it. The loudest woman was crying out, "Not John! No! God, why? Why, Father?"

She felt the blood leave her face. John? Something had happened to her son? She tried to take a step but she fell to her knees. Dirt and rocks shredded her skirt and dug into her skin. "John?" She called out his name and her voice became a scream. "What happened to John?"

She needed to get up. In her younger days she would've scrambled to her feet and run to the crowd. But the years held her back and without anyone to help her, she stayed on her knees, reaching out her hand. "What about my John?"

One of the young men in the group reached her first, the others moments behind him. "Elizabeth!" He stooped down and lifted her to her feet. "Are you okay?"

"What . . ." The colors around her melted together and spots circled before her eyes. She blinked hard, intent on staying alert. She grabbed hold of the young man's arm. "What happened . . . to my John?"

"Elizabeth, I'm so sorry." The man steadied her, his hands on her shoulders. "They killed him. Herod and his men."

She closed her eyes and shook her head. Not her John. She felt herself going down again. There had to be a mistake. "John!" she screamed with every bit of energy she had left. "Adonai, no! Please!"

This couldn't be happening. Somehow she was still on her feet. The group of people were holding her up. Someone had gotten a wet cloth and put it on her forehead, but that didn't stop the feeling consuming her — as if she were being dragged into the deepest, darkest tunnel. Falling . . . falling. She opened her eyes and in the distance she saw someone walking toward them, and then suddenly Elizabeth knew who it was.

It was Anne.

Her face looked stricken and as she reached the edge of the small crowd; someone must've told her what had happened because her hand flew over her mouth. Then Anne's eyes shifted and she looked straight at Elizabeth. And in that moment Elizabeth knew for sure.

Anne loved John. She always had.

Elizabeth felt the young woman's pain like a knife. The heartache was more than she could bear, but somehow she kept her eyes open long enough to see Zechariah coming up the road. He was too old to run, but clearly he could see the commotion. He moved as fast as he could.

She saw Zechariah stop the first person he came to, and, as with Anne, clearly that person told him the news. His face looked ashen and he limped, trance-like, toward Elizabeth. She had to stay awake, had to hold him before she let the pain take her. The spots were clouding her vision, but if the news was true, if their John had been killed, then she needed Zechariah.

Needed him like she needed her next breath.

Finally he was there, his still-strong arms around her. The other voices faded. "John's gone."

"Our son." Elizabeth couldn't cry, couldn't scream. The truth crashed in on her like so many rocks. Even in Zechariah's arms, it took all her strength to stand. "Not our son!"

She wanted to help Zechariah and Anne and the friends and family who were among the people gathered. But the black dots grew and Elizabeth could no longer hear anything but her broken, beating heart.

Why? God, why would You take our John? She wanted to ask Zechariah, look into his eyes and see some kind of answer, some reason to keep believing in the goodness of the God she had loved since she was a young child. But she could feel herself fading, falling into yesterday. Her last thought was of John . . . sitting in a prison cell alone.

She hadn't even said good-bye.

Elizabeth had wanted a baby for as long as she could remember.

But it didn't take long after she and Zechariah were married before she knew something was wrong. The expectation from her village and her family and especially her husband was that children would come soon after the wedding. Elizabeth expected that of herself.

Instead one month became two, and two months became a year.

That was the first time she and Zechariah had a serious talk about the matter. "I think it's me." She would never forget the pain in Zechariah's eyes that afternoon. "I'm sorry . . . Maybe I can't have children."

Despite telling her of his broken heart, Zechariah took her hands in his. "It's not your fault. With God all things are possible, Elizabeth. We will pray for a child and we will believe. As long as there is breath in our lungs."

Elizabeth wanted an answer, a way to fix things. But there was none. And so she had looked into her husband's eyes and allowed his faith to bolster her own. Seconds passed and then Zechariah bowed his head. "Let's pray to the Father."

So they had prayed.

They prayed as that year became two years, and then nearly twenty long years without a child. Elizabeth could still remember the Passover as Zechariah headed off to do his temple duties. He had felt something different, as if God was about to make Himself known like never before.

Elizabeth had prayed for him every day that week — as she promised she would. Still she was shocked when Zechariah came home without his voice. Mouthing words and making signs with his hands didn't help, but finally he found a way to communicate. The scrolls they still had in the corner of the house. A reminder of God's faithfulness.

It didn't take long before Zechariah explained what had happened. The angel Gabriel and the news about the baby and of course his disbelief, and the fact that he had been silenced. The news rattled in Elizabeth's barren heart for a few weeks. Then very early one morning she woke before sunup and climbed out of bed. She slipped outside and found a place to sit under the fading stars.

Peace settled around her uncertain soul and there in the quiet she knew. She absolutely knew. She was going to have a baby. A son. She put her hand over her stomach and watched the sun rise in the east. God hadn't forgotten them. And she knew something else, too.

This child would be special. God's hand would be upon him.

Elizabeth could only let herself go back, back to the year when John was born. And like that, she was holding her only child, and he was peering up at her with the most beautiful eyes, his hand wrapped around her finger.

"We have a son." Her voice was more cry than laugh. "Zechariah, look at him."

Her husband still couldn't talk, but the tears in his eyes said more than anything his words might've.

And it was time to present little John and then — only then — could Zechariah speak, and he was calling out to the family, "His name is John! His name has to be John."

From that day on everyone knew what Elizabeth and Zechariah had known from the beginning: God's hand was on their son.

He was special. Filled with the Holy Spirit. The angel had said that, and the proof was evident.

John was the best child, kind, courageous, and deeply aware of right and wrong. He loved to help but he also loved to listen. The images changed and John was eight years old, standing outside the house, apart from the other kids. His arms were crossed and he looked upset. Elizabeth walked out to him and put her hands on his sturdy shoulders. "What is it, John? What happened?"

"They were mean to Anne." He looked up at her, his eyes full of light. "No one should be mean, Mother."

"You're right. I'm sorry they did that." Elizabeth looked down the road toward Anne's house. "Was she crying?"

"Yes." He shook his head, clearly baffled. "It's like they can't tell when they hurt someone."

And Elizabeth was looking up at the distant hills and knowing the reason John felt that way. Because the Spirit of God was in him. The theme became recurrent, John obsessed with what was good and right and pure. His happiest moments were when Mary and Joseph brought their family each Passover.

Jesus and John.

Hadn't Elizabeth always known it would come down to that? She had felt John leap in her womb the moment Mary came to visit. Mary's son would be the Messiah, and Elizabeth's son would prepare the way for Him. What could be more exciting? The future looked as golden as any middle-eastern sunset.

But the sunset faded to dark and the memory vanished with it, and once more Elizabeth could hear voices around her.

"Elizabeth . . . are you okay?" It was Zechariah's voice. "Please open your eyes."

Only she didn't want to open her eyes because then it would be real again. Even with her eyes closed she remembered what had happened. John had been killed in prison. Her firstborn. Her only child. Her son. He was gone now.

Who was there to hold him as he died? Was it quick or did he suffer? Elizabeth began to cry. For the first time since the news hit her she allowed herself to feel. Her eyes stayed closed, but the hot tears slid down her weathered cheeks. John was gone.

Nothing would ever be right again.

The sounds quieted and she felt herself remembering a happier time. Zechariah had just found his voice and people were celebrating the miracle. And Zechariah began to praise their mighty God, the One who had given them a child in their later years. And Zechariah was singing. After nine months of silence he was singing a song that had been growing in his heart the whole time. Elizabeth was there again, quietly crying happy tears while Zechariah held a sleeping baby John in his arms.

But the part of Zechariah's song that played again in her heart was about John. That he would be called prophet of the Most High God and go ahead of the Lord to prepare the way for Him. Elizabeth had watched Zechariah hold a little more tightly to John as he kept singing. John would tell the people how they could be saved.

The miracle filled everyone in the room with wonder.

The images faded and only one thing consumed her. The end of Zechariah's song.

Because of the tender mercy of our God, by which the rising sun will come to us from heaven, to shine on those living in darkness . . . and in the shadow of death, to guide our feet into the path of peace.

At the time, those words seemed like a strange disconnect at the end of an otherwise happy song. Hopeful, but not altogether comforting. John had just been born. No need to sing about death.

Now, though, the words made perfect sense.

Kindness shining on those living in darkness . . . in the shadow of death. That was Elizabeth now. She was breathing still, but she had fallen into the darkness, beneath the shadow of death. The death of her precious John. Somehow God had told Zechariah even back then that they needed a plan for death.

Not *if* it came, but *when* it came.

As the reality hit her, Elizabeth felt herself coming to again, felt the awareness of John's murder like a searing iron against her soul. She could only beg God in the quiet, desperate places of her soul that the last line of Zechariah's song might also be true.

That peace might come because of God's kindness.

It was the only miracle left to pray for.

Somehow one day became the next. The sun kept rising and Elizabeth tried to remember how to breathe again. But every breath, every heartbeat reminded her of the truth, a truth that hung over her like a suffocating wet blanket.

Her John was dead.

Zechariah seemed to be fading since hearing the news. He hadn't gone to meet with the priests once in recent days, and his steps were slower than before. The two of them didn't say much, though often through the day he would find her and pull her into his arms. Just hold her because there were no words. The child sent to be a prophet, their son who loved right and hated wrong, had been murdered.

Elizabeth had developed a cough, and deep down she thought she might be seriously ill. Which would be a relief, compared to living with the knowledge that John was gone. That he'd never walk through the front door again. They had heaven to look forward to, eternity together. That was the one place where she still had hope. They would see each other again.

The morning felt warmer than usual. Zechariah was out back. Staring at the distant hills, the way he had a number of times since hearing about John's death. Elizabeth didn't feel like making bread, so she sat in the kitchen and stared out the door. John's memory was everywhere.

"God, give me hope," she whispered. "Help me get through this."

For a long time she sat without any sense of an answer. She tried to remember her last prayer before the news about John.

Hadn't her prayer been that John would be freed from prison and that she would see him again? Elizabeth let the question fill her mind. Yes. She had prayed it constantly, now that she was thinking more clearly.

A gentle breeze danced through the doorway and reminded Elizabeth that God's Spirit was still all around her. When she allowed herself to really process what had happened, she understood that God had answered her prayer. She stared outside at the wind in the far off trees. Yes, He had. John had indeed been freed from prison, and she would certainly see him again.

Just not the way she had planned.

The weight of his loss was still so heavy on her shoulders, in her heart. But for the first time since Herod's men had killed John, Elizabeth felt the stirrings of hope. God didn't always answer prayers the way His people expected. The way they intended. Clearly, Elizabeth wanted John released from prison here, wanted him back home in the kitchen where he could tell her about his time with Jesus, and the lonely days behind bars. But she couldn't argue with the fact that her prayers had been answered.

Elizabeth drew a deep breath and coughed a few times.

Someone was coming up the walk. Zechariah, maybe. Wondering what they were supposed to do next. How they were supposed to live again. Elizabeth stood to greet him, but instead of her husband, the person at the door was her cousin — Mary.

"Elizabeth." Her eyes were red from sadness. "I heard about John."

They embraced, and tears came for both of them. "You're here."

"Some of Jesus's disciples were headed this way. I traveled with them." She took hold of Elizabeth's hands. "I kept thinking back to the beginning. When I first knew I was pregnant. Our time together here." More tears filled her eyes. "I had to come."

"Did you ever think it would end like this?" Elizabeth looked straight at Mary, as if her cousin might somehow have the answers. "Back then . . . when angels were appearing to you and Zechariah and Joseph?"

"That's why I came." Mary thought for a while. "I think maybe I did know. I just never wanted to talk about it." She sighed. "As if talking about it might make it real."

This was news to Elizabeth, and she was suddenly desperate to understand what Mary meant. The idea that John was doomed to a violent ending was not something the two of them had ever discussed. Quite the opposite. Whenever they were together they dreamed of what these days with their grown sons would be like.

Elizabeth looked at her empty kitchen. "Help me make bread while we talk?"

"Definitely." Mary hesitated. "I've wanted to see you since I heard the news."

Elizabeth nodded. She could only hope something Mary was about to say could provide answers. Answers she desperately needed.

They walked into the kitchen and Mary pulled the vat of flour across the floor. "You look thin."

"I am." Elizabeth coughed a few times. "I might be sick." A sad smile lifted her lips. "I don't really care. Heaven looks very inviting from here."

"Mmm. I understand." Mary measured out the flour and yeast. "I taught Jesus about the yeast." Mary smiled. "Just as you taught me back then." Her eyes met Elizabeth's. "Jesus used what I taught Him in His teaching to the people. I think about it whenever I make bread."

"What does He teach about it?" Elizabeth welcomed the distraction, the chance to talk about something other than John's death.

"He compares the yeast to false teaching. It doesn't take much to ruin faith."

"Yes." Elizabeth could picture her nephew making that point.

They were quiet for a while, Mary measuring out the ingredients. Finally she took a deep breath. "What I never told you . . . It happened back when Jesus was just a baby. Joseph and I had taken Him to the temple and this older man named Simeon came to us."

Elizabeth leaned against the wall, already taken by the story. "Did you know him?"

"No." Mary stirred the flour and yeast together. "But he knew us. He said he was waiting for the consolation of Israel. Joseph and I could tell that the man had the Holy Spirit."

"What did he say?"

Mary's eyes held a distant look, as if she were back in the temple courts again and seeing the man Simeon for the first time. "He said the Spirit of God had told him he would not die before he had seen the Messiah. The Savior."

Chills ran down Elizabeth's arms. "And he knew it was Jesus?"

"Yes. He said God led him into the temple courts. As soon as he saw us he knew." Mary added water and olive oil to the flour mix.

"He ran to us and wanted to hold Jesus. It all happened so fast."

"I would've been nervous." Elizabeth found the baking pan and brought it to Mary. "A complete stranger, wanting to hold my baby."

"Exactly." Mary stirred the ingredients. She paused, clearly caught up in the memory. "The man began to praise God, announcing this proclamation over Jesus."

Elizabeth couldn't believe they had never talked about this before. "What did he say?"

"I can remember every word. He thanked God for keeping His promises, and for letting him see salvation before he died. How he was ready to go in peace now that he'd seen the Messiah. He said Jesus would be a light to the Gentiles and the glory of Israel." Mary paused and looked at Elizabeth. "I remember that."

"The Gentiles?" Elizabeth felt a pit in her stomach. "I can't imagine . . ."

"I know. That's how we felt. A little overwhelmed, that this man, this stranger, would know so much about our baby."

Mary kneaded the dough and they were quiet, the reality of the long ago meeting heavy on their hearts. Elizabeth spoke first. "How is Jesus?"

"Sad." Mary's emotions seemed to rise up

inside her. She struggled to talk. "After He got the news about John . . . He went away by Himself." She looked straight at Elizabeth. "He loved John. You know that."

Elizabeth nodded. Her thoughts were troubled, confused. "Jesus . . . He's still healing people? Giving the blind their sight?"

"He is. Everyone's talking about Him." Mary pursed her lips. "I know what you're thinking. I was there when Jesus raised Lazarus from the dead."

No words were needed. Elizabeth simply looked at Mary and waited.

"That's another reason why I had to come." Mary stopped kneading the dough and faced Elizabeth. "Jesus could've rescued John. He could've gotten him out of prison or brought him back to life. We both know that." Mary's voice trembled. "But something bigger is happening. It's something Simeon said at the end of our brief moment with him. That's the part I haven't wanted to think about."

The hurt in Elizabeth's heart felt fresh again. "What did he say?"

Mary closed her eyes for a few seconds before looking at Elizabeth. "He said Jesus would cause the falling and rising of many in Israel and that He would be spoken against. So that hearts might be revealed." Mary took a quick breath. "That part was difficult. But his last words were the worst."

Again Elizabeth waited, gripped by whatever might be coming.

"He said a sword would pierce my own soul, too."

"Too?" Elizabeth shuddered at the man's terrible prophecy.

"Yes . . . that's how he said it. A sword would pierce my soul, too."

Elizabeth felt sick. "That's awful. Jesus was just a baby."

"That's what I thought. Joseph had to comfort me for the next few days so I could finally stop thinking about it. But still . . . his words remain."

"As if . . ." Elizabeth didn't want to finish the sentence.

"As if something horrible was going to happen to Jesus — even though he didn't actually say that. And then something just as tragic would happen to me, too. What else could he have meant?"

No answers came to Elizabeth. Mary had to be right. Simeon seemed to have some special knowing. Otherwise he wouldn't have singled Mary and Joseph and baby Jesus out of the crowd. "Are people . . . upset with Jesus?"

Mary returned to kneading the dough. "Some." She covered the bowl and set it aside. Then she faced Elizabeth again. "The Pharisees and Sadducees, teachers of the law mostly. They understand who Jesus claims to be. He's telling people He's God in the flesh. The Savior whose coming was foretold." She paused. "It makes them mad."

Clouds had gathered outside, and a rumble of thunder shook the house. Mary waited until the sound passed. "Trouble is coming. I can sense it. Especially after what happened to John."

Elizabeth thought about that. "So you're saying if Jesus is destined for trouble, it was only fitting that John faced it first?"

"Maybe." Mary's eyes softened. "Before they killed John, Jesus was preaching. He told the crowds there has been no one greater born to women than John."

Tears gathered again in Elizabeth's eyes. "I . . . didn't know that."

"That's the other reason I had to come. So you wouldn't wonder about Jesus, how He felt about John."

Elizabeth closed her eyes and let the sadness rush over her again. She needed times like this, times to grieve and miss her only child. After a while, she dabbed at her eyes and lifted them to Mary's again. "Thank you."

"That same day, Jesus also said that the least important person in the kingdom of heaven was better than John." The passion in Mary's voice grew. "Because He knew that John wasn't going to be on earth much longer. He's in the better place. Jesus keeps trying to make that point whenever He teaches."

Rain started to fall outside, pelting the ground and the roof of the house. Elizabeth listened to the sound and sorted out what Mary had said. "So you're saying . . . Jesus didn't save John or bring him back to life because now . . ."

"He's home. He's really home. The place both of us long to be someday."

The message made more sense to Elizabeth than anything she'd heard in the last few days. As great as John had been, he was greater now. In the presence of the Father. Elizabeth felt relief. She leaned against the wall. "Thank you. For sharing that."

"I had to tell you." Mary nodded to the nearby chairs. "Let's sit down. You look tired."

"I am." Elizabeth followed her to the table and the two sat across from each other. She coughed again. "My lungs feel heavy."

"Your heart, too." Mary reached out and gave her hand a gentle squeeze. "I'm so sorry."

Elizabeth felt herself smile. "I feel better than I have since . . . since finding out. Knowing that John is greater now. I don't have to wonder why Jesus didn't rescue him or bring him back."

"John had finished what he was born to do." Mary's eyes were sad, despite her smile. "He prepared the way for Jesus." She leaned back. "That's another thing."

"What?" Elizabeth was grateful beyond words for Mary's visit.

"John prepared the way for Jesus." She hesitated. "But God has used you to prepare the way for me."

Elizabeth wasn't sure she understood. She leaned closer. "Me?"

"Yes." Mary had never looked more serious. "When the angel Gabriel visited me and told me I was going to have a baby, he pointed me to you. And so I came here."

That evening felt as though it had happened only yesterday.

Mary's expression grew more intense. "You prepared the way for Jesus's birth, Elizabeth. I needed to be here, to watch you go through it first. The pregnancy, the angel's promises . . . the delivery. I was here for it all." She took a breath. "Don't you see? You really did prepare the way for me."

"I never thought about it."

Tears welled in Mary's eyes again. "I was thinking about what Simeon said, all those years ago. How I would have pain, too." She hung her head for a moment, struggling to finish. "You showed me how to bring my baby into the world. What if . . . what if you are supposed to show me how to let Him go?"

The possibility made Elizabeth's head spin. "Mary, you think something's going to happen to Jesus?"

Her face looked stricken. "He keeps saying . . . He's going to be killed. And then raised to life on the third day. I used to think He was talking in parable. But then John was killed." Mary's voice fell to a whisper. "How do you do it, Elizabeth? How do you keep breathing?"

The reality of John's death rose once more to the surface of Elizabeth's broken heart. "I'm not good at it." Her eyes locked on Mary's. "You get up in the morning. You take one step and then another. Somehow you learn to inhale again."

Mary listened, her face drawn with sadness. "I think I needed to be here. So I could see for myself."

The truth filled Elizabeth with a purpose she hadn't considered before. The rest of the day and long after Mary left, the conversation replayed in her mind. It left her feeling lighter, more hopeful. Anxious for heaven. Because maybe Mary was right about Elizabeth's heartache. Her pain was not without purpose. God had chosen her to prepare the way for Mary in birth.

Now, just maybe, He had chosen her to prepare the way in death.

Elizabeth was worried about Zechariah. Weeks had passed since John's death, and now her husband hadn't eaten in days. He spent most of his time outside, looking into the sky or down at the stream behind the house. Oftentimes his grief was so great, tears coursed down his cheeks.

This was one of those times.

A few tight coughs wracked Elizabeth's body. It wouldn't be long now, not for her or Zechariah. But at least Elizabeth would live out the rest of her days certain that her pain had not been in vain. She had helped Mary for whatever was coming. At least that. She stepped to the doorway and looked out at Zechariah. He seemed lost in his own world of brokenness. So sad, so devastated.

Gradually, as Elizabeth watched him, the image before her eyes changed and she was no longer looking at her husband. Instead she could see John, when he was a boy, eight years old. He had been standing in the exact same spot looking over the valley behind their house, staring at the stream.

And he had been crying.

As if she were there again, Elizabeth could see herself hurrying to him, concerned for him. "John." She put her hands on his shoulders. "What's wrong, son? Why are you sad?"

And young John was looking up at her with those beautiful innocent eyes, and he was saying, "Why don't the kids love more, Mom? They don't understand about God and they don't love each other."

"Awww, honey, I'm so sorry." And she was comforting him, rubbing his back. "People need a Savior. We all do. Then we'll know more about love."

She watched determination work its way through her son's sorrow. "Well, then . . . I'll tell them, Mother. I'll tell them about love."

The sounds and smells and feel of the ground beneath her feet all changed in the blink of an eye and it was no longer John standing there, but Zechariah once more.

170

Her brokenhearted husband. Elizabeth moved toward him, her aging bones slow to close the distance. Zechariah needed her. When she finally reached him, she put her hands on his shoulders. "We'll see him again."

"I know." Zechariah breathed deeply and turned, facing her. His tear-stained, weathered face was the picture of grief. "Death isn't finished with our family. I've been thinking about Jesus."

"Mary and I talked about that, too. Jesus is next. The Scriptures and prophets have talked about that for generations." Fresh hope sounded in Elizabeth's voice. "But death won't have the last word. Jesus will live forever. Just like John." She kissed his cheek. "Like us."

Zechariah nodded slowly and once more he looked over his shoulder at the stream. "I loved that boy. I loved him so."

For a moment they both watched the stream, seeing images from yesterdays they could never live again. Finally Zechariah turned to her. "John did his job at the Jordan River." His eyes met hers again. "He told people to turn from their sins. He told them to be kind to one another and . . . he told them about Jesus."

"He always thought people needed to love

171

more." Elizabeth smiled, her tired eyes on the distant hills.

"Exactly."

"And now he's home. In the presence of the greatest love." She put her hands on either side of his face. "He finished his work."

"It was John's song, to tell people about Jesus."

"And now all eyes are on the Savior."

They came together in a hug, and Elizabeth knew her husband was going to be okay. In the days or weeks they had left on earth, he would remember what it was to believe and hope and look forward to tomorrow. Because John's job was finished. Now it was Jesus's time.

Jesus, Savior of the world.

The One mankind had been looking forward to since the dawn of creation. The Messiah sent to set His people free. And the Gentiles, too. Even them. One day soon all people would know of Jesus, and in the process they would know about John the Baptist.

Jesus's cousin and friend. Elizabeth and Zechariah's boy.

The one who had told the people about love.

STORY 5
JAMES
THE DOUBTING BROTHER

All of Nazareth was in an uproar and James was sick of it. His brother was acting insane, so maybe it was time to take action. James stepped outside his house and leaned against the doorframe. Jesus was having dinner down the street and even from this distance, James could see the multitudes, gathering around the dwelling, pushing their way inside.

"Jesus! Help us . . . Jesus, over here! Jesus, heal us!"

James watched through wary eyes.

Suddenly a man came screaming down the street, a child in his arms. "Let me through!" His eyes blazed with determination as he headed for the house where Jesus was. "We have to get to Jesus! Please, let us in!"

James scowled. This whole Jesus thing made absolutely no sense. James had watched Him grow up, after all. Jesus was the oldest of Joseph's sons. One of James's closest friends and constant companions. Until He left home and started telling people He was God.

Of all things.

James wiped the sweat off his brow and peered again at the distant chaos. It wasn't only the followers who were crowding the street, searching for Jesus. There were those who hated Him, too.

Not far from where James lived with his mother and brothers, a group of men anchored themselves to a spot on the street. The men shouted at the followers of Jesus, "He's a liar, not the Lord." They laughed and mocked those looking for Jesus. "Go home!"

Insanity. All because of James's big brother, Jesus.

A long sigh rattled in James's chest. Every time Jesus came through town, people picked sides. The sick, the lame, the down-and-out all clamored for His attention, looking for healing or some sort of inspiration. Jumping on the bandwagon. The others were just as loud. Family mostly. Cousins, aunts, uncles . . . people who knew the truth about Jesus.

He was the carpenter's son. He belonged to Mary and Joseph — not God. The son of

Joseph. Not the Son of God. And certainly not God in the flesh — the way His crazy disciples seemed to believe. If anyone knew the truth, James did. James, who had shared ten thousand breakfasts and lunches and dinners with his big brother.

Jesus had taught James everything He knew. About life and faith, work and wisdom. He was the best older brother a man could have. And then something made Jesus flip. He left home and became sick in His head.

James stepped back inside his doorway and furrowed his brow. He wasn't only fed up with Jesus, he was worried about Him. There was a murmur in the streets. Some people wanted Jesus killed for His claim. Jesus wasn't only embarrassing the family, He was risking His life. His and maybe the lives of His whole family. Maybe even their mother's life.

An idea took root in James's mind. Maybe it was time to put an end to the madness. James could go down the street and meet with Jesus, talk some sense into Him. He could get his mother and brothers to come along. Not that everyone in the family felt the way James did. Their mother probably believed Jesus's claims. But she didn't like hearing the rest of the family mock Him.

She would join them. Just to make sure they were kind to her precious Jesus.

"Oh, big brother . . . what's gotten into You?" A quiet chuckle came from James. The Savior of mankind — the Emmanuel spoken of in Isaiah — from a carpenter's son? In a town like Nazareth? He grabbed a flask of water, downed it, and slipped on his cloak. Yes, it was time. Enough was enough. He'd give it an hour, wait till the house down the street was full of people. Then he and his family would act.

They had to.

James stood outside and watched the people stream toward the house. If only he could turn time around, find a way back to how things used to be. He closed his eyes for a minute and willed himself to remember, all the way down yesterday's road to the beginning.

James could picture the day Jesus set out from home the first time. James had been looking for his brother and he found Him in the carpenter's shop. It was a day he would never forget. Jesus had been quiet all afternoon. Finally James went looking for Him. Sure enough, He was in the family work area. Only this time He wasn't working late — as He sometimes did.

He was packing.

"Jesus?" James entered the room slowly. "What are You doing?"

"It's time." Jesus had set down His things and looked at James. Right through him. No one had kinder eyes than Jesus.

James came closer and sat at the table. An uneasy fear worked through him. "Time for what?"

"My calling. The reason I'm here." Jesus returned to filling His bag. Gentle finality rang in His voice. "All My life has led to this."

James searched for something to say. Was Jesus headed to Jerusalem? He had always liked trips to the temple — maybe that was it. James found the words. "How long . . . will You be gone? More than a few days?"

Again Jesus looked up. "For good. Until they take My life."

"Jesus." The room began to bow and bend and James felt his heart hit the floor. "Don't talk like that. No one will take Your life. You're . . . You're the most liked man in all of Nazareth. Everyone says —"

"James." Once more Jesus looked deep into James's eyes. "This will happen as I say. The way it is written about Me."

They sat in silence for a few minutes and then an understanding had hit James.

Maybe something was wrong with Jesus. He could've hit His head or fallen ill. Moving discreetly so as not to alarm his brother, James left the shop and ran to find their mother.

"Something's happened to Jesus."

"What?" His mom's face showed instant alarm. She grabbed the sleeve of James's tunic. "Where is He?"

"In the shop. He's packing His things. He said He's leaving." James hesitated, not sure how much he should tell her. "Mother, He said He's leaving for good."

The news seemed to hit their mother slowly, like a series of carefully aimed arrows. She moved to the nearest wall and leaned against it, as if it was the only thing stopping her from falling to the floor. "Did . . . He say anything else?"

Confusion worked its way through James's being. "Doesn't that shock you? I mean, Mother, Jesus can't leave! He runs the shop. We all need Him."

Mary blinked a few times. "Did He say anything else?"

"Yes." James thought for a second. "He said it was time for His calling. That all His life had led to this."

A faraway look filled their mother's eyes and she stared out the window. "His time."

James wasn't sure what that meant. But if Jesus was losing His mind, then maybe James better tell her the rest. He steadied himself. "He said something else."

Mary looked at him, waiting.

"He said He was leaving until . . . they take His life."

His mother's eyes closed and she turned her face to the wall. "No."

"That's what I told Him. I said He couldn't go, and that no one was going to hurt Him." James went to his mother and took a gentle hold of her arm. "Mom, He told me that everything written about Him had to take place." He paused, letting that sink in. "What could make Him say something like —"

"He is right." Mary opened her eyes and again she looked out the window. "Jesus is not like you or me, James. He came from God."

"What?" James released his mother's arm. He stared at her for a long moment and then paced the kitchen. "Do you hear yourself? Jesus is your son, Mother. He's special, yes. But He didn't come from God. He and I have the same father, the man you loved who —"

"That's enough." His mother rarely raised her voice, but this was one of those times.

"We must let Him go. I've known this was coming . . . since Jesus was born."

James was troubled before, but now he was desperately upset. "I can't believe you're taking His side. Like this is some sort of normal event."

"It's as Jesus said. Everything written must take place."

James had nothing more to say. He left his mother's side and went to find his brothers. They would certainly understand. At least with them he had a sympathetic audience.

"Of course Mother understands about Jesus," their youngest brother had said. "He's been her favorite from the beginning. That's no secret."

It was true. James had enjoyed having Jesus as his older brother, but now that he thought about it, Jesus could do no wrong. He had the perfect response whenever their mother needed help, and He knew the Scriptures as if He'd spent His whole life memorizing them. He was so nice to the other kids when they were little that no one could say a bad thing about Him.

Despite all that, James had never been jealous of Jesus. But the way their mother defended Him made him struggle with an unfamiliar envy. "I mean, He's been perfect. I'll give Him that." James had felt his frustration growing. "But sent from God? That's taking this whole thing too far." He motioned for his brothers to come closer. "I have a plan."

And so the brothers made a pact to do what they could to stop Jesus from leaving. But one at a time as they approached Him, He told them the same thing He told James. There was no changing Jesus's mind. The time had come for Him to leave.

They shared a final meal together, though most of the family said very little. When the dinner was over, Jesus pulled James aside. "Listen, I promised Dad I'd take care of Mom. I'll be around. And she may travel with Me at times. But for now I need that to be your job — caring for her."

James nodded, dazed. "You're serious? You're really leaving?"

"I am." Peace emanated from Jesus's face and voice. "Tell Me you'll watch after Mom."

"Of course." He hesitated. As ridiculous as this was, James still adored Jesus. "I'd do anything for You, Jesus. Anything for her."

"Good." Relief filled His eyes. "We will see each other again."

"Of course."

From that moment until early the next day when Jesus left, James did everything he could to convince himself Jesus wasn't really going to leave. It was a phase, certainly. A whim. Jesus would go and wander about for a few days or even a few weeks. But then He'd come home and everything would go back to the way it was.

Even as Jesus walked away, James had believed he was right. Jesus would return and they could put the whole matter behind them.

But Jesus never did. He never even looked back.

From the beginning He began telling crowds of people this ludicrous story about His being the Messiah. God in the flesh. The sad thing was that James had always believed Jesus was the greatest guy — until now. When they were kids, as far as James was concerned, Jesus could walk on water.

Until Jesus said that He actually could.

Some of His disciples even claimed to have seen it happen! On the Sea of Galilee in the middle of a storm. On top of the water.

The first time Jesus came home after He set out on this pointless journey, James tried to casually approach the situation. "Come on, Jesus . . . we miss You. Don't You think it's time to stop traveling?" James had given Jesus a light slap on the shoulder. "I need

You, Brother. You and me . . . like it used to be. Mom needs You, too."

But Jesus had only looked at him — with that same unconditional love He'd always had for James. A smile even tugged at His lips. "I have to go. It's what My Father has called Me to do." His smile fell a little. "It's My calling. James . . . I know you don't understand. But you will one day."

Another time when Jesus was home, some of the locals were so angry at Him they chased Him to a cliff at the edge of town and were about to push Him off. James had run to the scene as fast as he could. He didn't believe Jesus's claims about being God, of course, but he would've fought anyone who tried to hurt his brother.

By the time James reached the edge of town, Jesus had escaped. No one really knew how. Later people talked about how Jesus had said, "It's only in His hometown that a prophet is without honor."

A prophet? James hadn't understood any of it. What was Jesus trying to prove? James had figured someday soon Jesus would be His old self, and they could go on being a family: Making memories and sharing meals. Working in the shop. James and his best friend, Jesus.

His big brother.

But Jesus had continued spinning His assertions until now the situation was out of control. For months Jesus had been traveling throughout the entire region, claiming to heal people and drive out demons. All sorts of nonsense. However He was pulling off the trickery, His actions were causing people to believe He was the Messiah.

Not only had Jesus's story gotten further from the truth, but something else had happened. Jesus seemed to have forgotten about James. His very own brother. James looked down the street again. Jesus was right here in town and He hadn't even stopped by the house. What sort of calling would take Him away from the people He loved most? Jesus's outrageous beliefs had destroyed any connection they'd had. And now it had led to this.

The raucous madhouse down the street.

The hour passed and finally it was time. James couldn't wait a moment longer. He walked off the hot, dusty street back into the house and shut the door behind him. Ten minutes later he had gathered his brothers and hatched a plan.

They would stay in a tight group, push their way through the crowd to the front door of the house, and tell the owner that

Jesus's family needed a word with Him. Then with loud, dramatic discussion, they would fully and finally put Jesus in His place.

With everyone listening.

James and the brothers were talking about who would speak first when their mother walked in. She looked from James to the others. "What's all this?"

"We're going to talk to Jesus." James looked at his brothers for support. "He's hurting Himself and us. All this talk about being the Savior." James took a step toward her. "Mother, He's out of His mind. You know that."

Mary said nothing. She lifted her chin ever so slightly and looked at each of her sons. "I've told you before. Jesus is from God. He is special."

"Yes." James tried to be patient. "We know He's special. But He's taken the whole thing too far. People have already tried to kill Him." He paused so his mom could feel the full weight of his next words. "One day they're really going to do it if He keeps this up."

The expression on their mother's face changed. Where there had been peace, now there was fear. She drew a long breath and steadied herself. "Maybe you're right." Her words held a caution. "If you're kind . . . if you ask Him gently . . . maybe He might come home."

Relief flooded James. "Exactly." He waited, letting the idea settle in his mother's heart. "So, you're with us?"

"We must be respectful." She looked at each of her sons again. "We don't want to embarrass Him. Not in any way."

"Definitely not." James could almost see Jesus sitting around their table again, laughing about the day's work. He took hold of Mary's hand. "We should go now, Mother. Before things get any more out of hand."

The youngest of the brothers spoke up. "This is the right decision. We need to put the idea to rest — Jesus the Messiah." He stood and took his place on the other side of their mother. "We have an obligation not only to Jesus, but to the townspeople — to tell them the truth."

Mary nodded. Her eyes looked distant again. "I . . . don't want anyone to hurt Him."

"It's the only way," one of his brothers agreed. "The kindest thing we can do for the people of Nazareth . . . and for Jesus."

With that Mary nodded. "Let's be quick. I don't want to make a scene."

"Come with us?"

"Yes." She straightened her garments. "Let's go."

And so they set out. James and the brothers, and their mother, Mary. On the walk down the street, a mix of anger and sorrow seized James. How could his relationship with Jesus have come to this? Where had that brother disappeared to? How had He grown so callous toward His family? Maybe the move they were making now would change everything.

They kept walking.

James wiped the dust from his face and mouth as they reached the house. "Let us through. We're His family!" James used his loudest voice. "We need a word with Jesus! Please, get out of the way."

"Be kind," their mother whispered. Her voice held a desperate urgency. "Please, James."

"I am." James turned forward again. "This is the best thing I can do."

They pushed their way to the front door. Someone looked them up and down. "Can I help you?"

"We are Jesus's family." James spoke with authority. "Please. We need to speak to the master of the house."

The man was gone for several minutes and then another man came to speak to them.

"Yes? This is my house." He looked bewildered. "You want to talk to Jesus?"

"We do." James took the lead. He stuck out his chest. "Tell Him His mother and brothers have come."

The man was gone for less than two minutes. When he returned, he shook his head. "I'm sorry. Jesus says He cannot talk."

James felt his mother grab his arm. But he wouldn't back down. This was his idea. He couldn't fail her. James took a step closer to the man. "What's that supposed to mean? This is Nazareth. Everyone knows Jesus is our family. He's my brother." James turned and nodded at Mary. "This is His mother. Now, please . . . step aside."

The man hesitated and shot a quick glance at a few of the people in the house. Several of them came closer, blocking the door along with the master. "I'm sorry. Jesus is busy."

"That's unacceptable." James could feel his anger rising. "Tell Him we absolutely must speak to Him."

Sweat formed on the man's brow. He wiped his palms on his cloak. "Jesus gave me a message for you." The man was clearly uncomfortable. "He said . . . His mother and brothers are those who . . . hear His word and obey it."

James felt his face grow hot. His heart pounded within him and the words and voices swirled around him. Nothing made sense and for a moment he thought he might pass out.

Again the man shook his head. "I'm sorry. I must go." And with that he shut the door.

James and his brothers and mother stood outside, along with hundreds of other people who hadn't gotten into the house. James could feel the eyes of everyone on him. People stared and a few even snickered. James could feel his mother's hand on his shoulder.

"We need to leave." Her words were soft, but firm. "Come, James. There's nothing more for us here. Nothing we can do."

James could barely breathe. Jesus had completely and utterly rejected them — His very own family. James hesitated, but then he followed Mary through the crowd. He had never been more embarrassed. Jesus had publicly disowned them.

They left in quiet shame. The whispers and stares of half of Nazareth followed them all the way back to their house. Not until they had closed the door behind them did James find the strength to put words to his feelings. "How . . . could He do that?"

"Now we know." Another brother had an

angry tone. "Jesus has completely changed."

"He never would've done this before." The youngest brother spoke up, his voice loud. "It's as if . . . He never knew us. Never loved us."

Their voices rose, the anger gaining ground among them. They rehashed the events, getting more upset with every passing moment. The whole time their mother said nothing. She only watched them, taking it in.

"Maybe it's time we disown *Him*!" James punched his fist into the palm of his hand. "Maybe out in the open. Where everyone can see how we feel about this."

Mary shook her head slowly. Indignation filled her expression and she held up her hand. "Stop."

"I'm sure if we called a meeting with the town leaders we could —"

"I said stop!" Mary looked at James, her eyes flashing. "That's enough." She turned to the brothers standing around. Her hands shook and gradually she lowered her voice. "We will stand by Jesus — privately and publicly."

She walked around the room and touched each of her sons on the shoulder, making eye contact. "Whatever Jesus says, whatever He does, He is my son. And He is your brother. We will stand by Him as long as I live."

She turned to James. "I know you mean well, son. But please . . . I need you to get on with your life." Their mother personified kindness. "Let Jesus be."

James nodded. If it weren't enough to be publicly shunned at the house down the street, now his mother had put him in his place. In front of all his brothers. James had never been more devastated. He took hold of his mother's hand for a moment. "I will respect your wishes. I just . . . I need time alone."

The sun had set and a few stars dotted the sky as James walked behind his family's house. He found a quiet spot and lifted his eyes to the shadowy hills beyond their home. *You promise help to those who call out to You. Well . . . I'm calling out now, Father. Something has happened to Jesus. He . . . doesn't love us anymore. If You could please help me be patient with Him. And please, bring my brother back around, Father. I don't care if everyone in town laughs at me. I miss Him.*

Tears stung James's eyes. He waited, looking to the heavens, but no answer came. No purposeful or confident response spoke to the quiet of his soul. James drew a few deep breaths. Nothing. His mother was right. They had no choice but to stand by Jesus — even now.

And maybe . . . maybe one day Jesus would come back.

James wanted to forgive Jesus, but instead he stayed angry through summer and into fall . . . that year and the next. Their cousin John became a very outspoken follower of Jesus, a decision that cost him his life.

As time passed, James's anger was exceeded only by his sorrow. He never could've imagined Jesus — the one who loved him the most — doing this to him, to their family.

Not until Passover that year did James catch wind that things weren't going so well for Jesus. It was their mother who convinced them that maybe it was time for a reconciliation. By then she had been traveling with Jesus, like one of His followers. "We're going to Jerusalem," she told them. "If we can see Him, we should. I love Him and I miss Him. I know you all do, too." She paused, her heart clearly heavy. "Jesus is in trouble. He needs us."

It was a quiet trip to the city, and along the way James caught himself torn by his conflicting emotions. The anger and rejection, the sense of betrayal Jesus had brought by His actions that awful time at the house. But also a simmering fear . . . because the closer they got to Jerusalem, the more they heard the murmurings.

The people of Israel wanted to kill Jesus.

Heated tension, mobs of angry Israelites, people refusing the claims of Jesus: everywhere James and his mother and brothers went, things grew worse.

And then it happened.

Jesus was arrested and all around Jerusalem people were talking. One of His friends had betrayed Him. Now Jesus had been captured because of His claims about being the Savior. Soldiers were reportedly beating Him, whipping and mocking Him. James was deeply troubled over the news. Especially since he had seen this coming years ago.

"If He would've listened to us that night at the house, none of this would've happened." James sat with his mother. "The Jews know what Jesus is saying, Mother. He's claiming to be God. It's going to get Him killed."

"We are His family." Tears filled her eyes. "We will pray for Him and support Him."

There was no choice after that. James wanted to burst through the prison and grab

Jesus, apologize for His wild claims and get Him home. Safe. Before they killed Him. Instead James could do nothing but stay with their mother and try to comfort her. The way several of Jesus's disciples and followers stayed to comfort each other.

When morning came, the news was worse. The Roman officials planned to make the Jewish people a deal. They could have Jesus or a convicted killer — Barabbas. James had a sickening feeling that the people would rather save a criminal than a man claiming to be the Christ.

James couldn't stand still. He paced and prayed and looked toward the place where Pontius Pilate would eventually appear. And as the day wore on, sure enough, the deal transpired. Pilate made the offer: Jesus or Barabbas. James and the brothers stood with Mary and the followers of Jesus as the crowd began to chant: "Barabbas! Barabbas! Barabbas!"

Pilate looked worried — and for a moment James felt a flicker of hope. But then Pilate looked to the people to answer the next question. "What should I do with Jesus of Nazareth?"

"Crucify Him!" They cried the words over and over again.

With each vicious shout, James watched

his mother collapse a little more.

Pilate raised his arms and stilled the crowd. Then he took a basin of water and washed his hands. "This man's blood will not be on me, but on you." With that, the decision was made.

Jesus was to be handed over and crucified.

"No!" His mother's scream was lost in the melee, but James heard it. She was suddenly frantic, rushing to her feet and pushing toward the place where Jesus was being kept. "Please, James," she cried. "I need to see Jesus . . . tell Him I love Him . . . just one more time. I have to get to Him. Jesus!"

If James could've taken his mother to Jesus, he would've done so immediately. But there was no way now. Jesus was locked up, guarded by armed soldiers. The decision had been made. Jesus would be crucified later that day. His crime, the one James feared would eventually be Jesus's undoing: His claim to be King of the Jews. Jesus the Messiah. He had taken the whole act too far, and now He was going to die because of it.

With his arm around Mary, James leaned close so she would hear him. "We can't go to Him. But we can find a spot on the road, follow Him to Golgotha."

"I need to be with Him, James. Please . . . help me find a way. He's the Messiah, no matter what anyone says."

James froze in place. "What?"

Even in the noise of the crowd, his mother spoke loud enough to be heard. "He is the Messiah. I've known that since before He was born."

This was the final blow. "You've believed Him all along."

"Yes." His mother didn't break eye contact. "Even when I wanted to doubt Him, to protect Him, I believed. Of course I believed. He isn't from this world."

One of Jesus's followers put his hand on Mary's shoulder. "We need to get to the road. Come on, Mary."

She nodded but kept her attention on James. "Are you coming?"

"No." He had to draw the line somewhere. "I am not one of His followers."

His mother looked intently at him. "Jesus is the Savior. He is God in the flesh, James." She put her hand alongside his face. "The angel told me before Jesus was born. He is God. He always has been."

The sorrow in his mother's eyes nearly broke his heart. But James couldn't stay with her. Their own mother might believe Jesus's claims, but James would not. And he wouldn't feel compelled to pretend.

He'd had enough.

James planned to go back to the place where they were staying in Jerusalem. But when he was twenty yards away from the crowd, he changed his mind. He could follow along at a distance, right? See how things played out. Amidst the chaos James even saw John — one of the disciples who had abandoned Jesus. Apparently he had come back and now he walked alongside James's mother.

The frustration in James doubled. He walked at a distance parallel to the crowd, staying to the outer edge, and from there he could see Jesus clearly, bloodied and beaten, carrying an enormous wooden cross.

Even from a distance, James heard his mother cry out along the way: "Someone stop this!" She reached toward the place where Jesus was passing by. "Jesus is innocent!"

James wanted to add his voice to the mix. Where was the justice in all this? Jesus might've been mad, but He wasn't dangerous. He'd done nothing worthy of the death penalty. The small band of supporters moved quickly, pushing their way through the throng of people, but James stayed apart from the group. As in Jesus's life, the crowd was split — some wailed, begging the soldiers to have mercy. Others mocked Jesus, demanding His crucifixion.

This far from Nazareth no one recognized James moving along by himself, no one pointed and stared at him because he was related to Jesus. But as the crying around him grew, James was no longer sure he cared whether people mocked him or not. His mother was right: this was a time to stand up for Jesus. Regardless of the strange things He believed.

But James couldn't bring himself to move closer.

Jesus's disciple, John, was caring for his mother, so she didn't need James right now. The farther they walked, the closer they came to the place where Jesus would be crucified. Suddenly James knew he couldn't be angry or upset with Jesus for another moment. The reality was setting in: his brother . . . his best friend . . . was about to be killed on a cross.

In the chaos of the early afternoon James talked to God quietly and frantically. *We need a miracle, Father. Don't let Him die. Please bring a rescue, Lord. Give us a way out.* Closer to crowd, James could hear his mother praying the same way. When her eyes weren't on Jesus, they were on the sky above the madness. The tears on her cheek were proof of her desperation.

Finally, the procession made its way to Golgotha at the town's end, the place where executions were staged. James climbed to the roof of a low-slung building and crawled to the edge. He lay there on his belly, until he was sure no one had seen him. Then he stood behind a chimney, and peered around the side. From that vantage point he could see it all — the soldiers stopping Jesus and laying the cross down on the ground. And Mary and John and the other followers standing not far away.

The crowd was getting louder, their hateful words toward James's brother almost deafening. Haters spit and shouted at Him. A few wailed on His behalf. James kept his eyes on Jesus. He'd been stripped of most of His clothes, His body battered and bloodied. The soldiers threw Him down on top of the cross.

Suddenly the sun's light faded and darkness came over the land. James looked around, his heart pounding. All of Jerusalem was nearly dark as night.

"Jesus . . . No! Please, someone help Him!" their mother cried out, her hands stretched out. Her cry cut through the sound of the crowd. "Let Him go! He's my son!"

For a single moment Jesus turned and looked at their mother. The connection was electric. Without saying a word He made it clear that He was somehow okay, even accepting His death willingly. He said it all with just a look. James studied his mom. She seemed stronger than just a few minutes earlier. Brokenhearted, yes. But the exchange with Jesus had breathed life into her countenance, no question.

Then just as quickly Jesus turned His eyes up to James. All the way to the rooftop where James was hiding behind the chimney. The look lasted only a second or two, but James could see something he had doubted for the past few years: no matter their differences, Jesus loved Him. In that moment of connection James no longer cared about Jesus's belief in the whole Messiah story. This was his brother, the one he had lost.

The one about to die.

James thought about scrambling back to the ground and running to help Jesus. He had to do something, right? James moved back to the edge of the roof, but at the same time the soldiers held Jesus's wrist to the horizontal bar of the cross and drove a stake straight through it.

"Jesus!" James cried out. He couldn't help Him now. It was too late. James clutched his stomach, sick with grief as he made his way back to the spot near the chimney.

Their mother was crying again, her eyes never once leaving Jesus. Sometimes her prayers could be heard above the crowd. "Help Him, God! Rescue Him!"

But the soldiers were unrelenting with Jesus and the two criminals set to be crucified on either side of Him. Each cross bore a sign stating the crime for which the man was being killed. James squinted up at Jesus's sign. *Jesus of Nazareth, King of the Jews,* it read.

That was all.

The noise from the crowd grew and swirled into a horrifying screech that sounded like hell itself. Their mother looked away as the last two stakes were driven through Jesus's wrist and feet. Jesus's scream cut through the sound of the crowd.

James wanted to look away but he could not. Surely God wouldn't let Jesus be killed this way. James closed his eyes. What was happening? Where was God when they needed Him? He blinked his eyes open and shook his head. He couldn't talk, couldn't draw a full breath. Jesus was dying. Right before their eyes He was slipping away.

James wept with an angry hopelessness. Before Jesus took His final breath, He looked for several seconds at their mother. Then He looked to John and back to Mary again. In a voice loud enough for all of them to hear Jesus cried out, "Dear woman, here is your son!"

Shock ran through James's veins. *John? The follower of Jesus?* He wasn't Mary's son. From his place on the rooftop, James steadied his shaking knees as Jesus turned to John again. "Here is your mother."

John nodded. Even as Jesus finished speaking, John moved closer to Mary and put his arm around her.

Suddenly James remembered what Jesus had asked him to do before He left home three years ago: *Take care of Mom.* That's all He'd wanted. James had tried to do that, but here . . . now . . . he wasn't with her. He wasn't standing at her side helping her. That job had fallen to John, and now Jesus had handed over care of their mother to him, His friend and follower.

James wanted to shout at Jesus, tell Him that he could take care of their mother without anyone's help. But suddenly he understood. Jesus wanted their mother cared for by someone who stood by her. The way John did. Someone who believed in Him.

Someone who followed Him.

Death was claiming Jesus, His breaths waning. But James felt like the victim. His brother had abandoned them and given His life for His strange beliefs. And now He had taken their mother from him. None of it made sense. The hurt in James's heart was beyond words, beyond movement. As if the cross were claiming his own life right alongside that of his brother.

Time passed in pain and disbelief, the details and sounds and sights blurring together in James's heart and mind. Finally from the cross Jesus called out His final words: "Father, into Your hands I commit My Spirit." He gasped. "It is finished!"

With that He bowed His head and the struggle left His body. His followers cried out, calling to God for help. James could do nothing but join them — even from a distance. No matter how much Jesus's actions had hurt him, the finality was almost more than James could take.

Jesus was dead.

Every wonderful time, every childhood memory played again in his mind and he wondered if he would survive the pain. Jesus had always been there for him when they were growing up. Now, James wanted to be there for Jesus. But he could do nothing. Nothing at all.

James needed to be with his mother. He turned to climb down off the roof, but when he was halfway to the ground, the earth began to shake . . . a menacing, terrifying earthquake. All around him people began to scream, and suddenly the ground split open and there was a terrible sound.

Like everyone else, James turned to see what thing might make such a noise. Everywhere he looked bodies were coming out of the nearby tombs. Walking out alive. Only later would they learn that at the moment of Jesus's death, the curtain of the temple was ripped in two — from the top down. Priests would describe it later, as if invisible hands were tearing it in half.

As if God Himself had destroyed it.

Then, in a rush like wind through a canyon in a sudden storm, the truth came upon James: Jesus had been right! He had been right all along. The miracles . . . all of them had been true stories — not fables. He really *had* walked on water. In the distance James heard one of the soldiers call out, "Surely, this was the Son of God."

Jesus was God. The Messiah. The Savior.

His brother was the One written about in Scriptures. The One come to save the world. This is what Jesus meant when He said everything written about Him had to be fulfilled.

Every word, everything Jesus ever claimed. All of it was true.

The piercing pain of the reality ripped through James in a way that nearly killed him. Jesus was God. But for James it was too late. Too late to tell Jesus he had changed his mind. Too late to apologize or tell Jesus he believed now. Too late to make things right. James buried his face in the dirt and cried out. "Forgive me . . . please, Jesus . . . forgive me!"

He had lost his brother. But more than that he had denied his God. And in the process James had lost his mother and his self-respect. What sort of worthless man was he, denying Jesus? Of course Jesus had been telling the truth. His brother had never lied in all His life. James wanted just one more moment with Jesus, to tell Him he was sorry and hug Him — the way they used to hug. One chance to acknowledge that Jesus was God in the flesh.

But it was too late for James.

And he would spend the rest of his life regretting the fact.

The days melted together for James in a dark and painful montage of memories and self-hatred. If only he had it to do over again. He would've been by Jesus's side every minute of the last three years. He would've been in the front row for the miracles and walked with Him from village to village the way their mother had.

On and on, the regrets continued.

Finally it was Sunday, the first day of the week. James was at the place where his family was staying for Passover, wishing for one more hour with Jesus when he heard a sound behind him. With a start, he turned and though the door remained locked, there stood —

"Jesus!" James stood unmoving, shocked. "Jesus, You're alive!" He had risen from the dead — just as His followers believed would happen. Just as He talked about doing before He was crucified. With trembling legs, James went to Him. He fell to his knees and hung his head. "Forgive me, Jesus . . . please . . . I was wrong."

"James." Jesus hesitated until James lifted his eyes. "Look at Me. The real Me."

James did as he was told. He lifted his

head and for a long time he looked into the eyes of Jesus. Never in all his life had James felt such love, sensed such grace and mercy. The nail marks were still there in His hands, but Jesus was clearly only focused on one thing.

James.

"Stay, Jesus . . . Live with the family." James brought his hands together, pleading. "It can be like it was." But even as he said the words he knew the answer.

"I cannot stay." Jesus smiled, his voice warm with compassion.

James struggled to his feet and for the most wonderful moment the two of them looked at each other. Like old times. "You will always be My brother, James." Jesus stepped back. "But now you will be My disciple. And you will lead My church in Jerusalem."

"Yes, my Lord." James bowed and their eyes met once more. "I will serve You all the days of my life."

Jesus smiled. And with that . . . He was gone. With Him went every bit of regret and defeat. All of James's discouragement and doubt. He could breathe again. He could look forward to tomorrow.

James filled his lungs and thought about the miracle he'd just witnessed. Jesus loved him enough to come see him. Just him. He must've known that James was suffocating with guilt.

But not anymore.

Life filled his bones as James stood. Then and there he vowed to keep his promise. He would serve Jesus forever. He would tell stories of the Messiah and lead people to follow His teachings. He would do so every day, all the while remembering their times as children . . . and this — their final meeting. Because until the end of His earthly life, Jesus had been his brother . . . his best friend. But now He was so much more.

Now Jesus was his God.

STORY 6
MARY
THE LOVING MOTHER

John the Baptist had been dead for a few weeks, and from a distance, Mary watched her son grieving the fact. With all her heart she wished just one thing.

That Joseph was still alive.

Her love, her strength, her husband. Joseph would've known what to say to help Jesus through these tough times. Joseph had always been so protective and capable. Especially when life got crazy. In his absence, Mary did the only thing she could do since Joseph died. She prayed for Jesus. When she didn't know how to help her son, she asked God to help.

Which He always did.

Prayer was the most Mary could do for Jesus. She couldn't care for Him or protect Him or give Him advice. She was His follower now, but she would always be His mother. Which was why she had gone to see Elizabeth. She'd been back for a couple of days, and she felt stronger for their time together. Mary understood better now how life could go on.

Even after a son had been killed.

The details of John's death were gruesome. Mary knew more than she had shared with Elizabeth. Jesus knew, too. How Herodias's daughter had gotten her wish: John's head on a platter. After his murder, John's followers, including one of Herod's guards, came and tended to his body, placing it in a tomb. Bringing some dignity to his death.

As long as she lived she would never forget what happened when Jesus heard the news. Now, while Jesus taught in the distance, Mary pondered all that had taken place around Him in the wake of John's murder. The memory played in her mind as if it were happening again.

Jesus had heard the news the day after John had been killed. Mary was one of the followers with Him and she had watched Him turn and bring His hands to His face for a few seconds. Then He lifted His eyes to heaven. After a minute, He turned back to His disciples. Mary could still see the way His face looked, the grief in His eyes as He spoke. "I need to be alone."

No one could blame Him. He'd been

healing people and driving out demons, teaching about the kingdom of God without rest for such a long time. But in that instant, with His cousin beheaded because of Him, Jesus knew what He needed.

Time alone with His Father.

So Mary and the others watched Him climb into a boat and sail to a quiet place by Himself.

"Let's follow Him!" one of the men had cried out. "We can walk around the lake and meet Him on the other side."

In no time the disciples and followers began the walk around the lake and along the way others joined them. It took a day and night, but eventually — early the next morning — they reached a spot on the other shore where they could see Jesus's boat.

The crowd pressed closer, everyone wanting something from Jesus. Mary wanted only one thing — to see her son. In case He needed food or water after His time on the boat. But before she could reach Him, Jesus was ashore, healing the sick and teaching, His voice filled with compassion.

Mary knew how tired Jesus had to be, but it didn't matter. Everywhere He turned there was another crippled child or suffering woman or man. Jesus loved them all — that much was clear. At one point Jesus looked at Mary. Straight at her, as if He always knew where she was, no matter how many people were gathered around Him. Their eyes met — the way they had countless times before — and in that simple exchange Mary knew her son was okay. He was doing what He was born to do, with a strength that came from God alone.

He was not only the Savior, He was God in the flesh. For that reason He could accomplish anything He wished.

Jesus's teaching that day went from morning to late afternoon. Mary remembered what happened next — the way they would all remember it. His disciples came to Him, concerned and a little irritated. Mary couldn't see which of the men was talking, since they had their backs to her. They had come to Him as a group. But Mary could hear their words: "There is nothing to eat here," they said. "It's already getting late. Send the crowds away."

A chorus of agreement came from the others. "That's right," one said. "They can go and buy food in the villages!"

Jesus looked at the disciples, His eyes warm with patience and understanding. Finally He smiled. "They don't need to go away. You give them something to eat."

Even from her place a ways behind the

disciples, Mary could feel their disbelief. "We have only five loaves of bread and two fish!" one of them cried out. "Have You seen the crowd?"

Again compassion flooded Jesus's voice. He spoke slowly, in no hurry. "Bring them to Me."

At first it looked as if the disciples might argue. After a few seconds, they shuffled off and returned with the five loaves and two fish.

Jesus took the food, stood on a hillside, and called out to the people, "Please, take a seat in the grass. We are going to share a meal."

The area was packed full of people, so it took a while. Eventually, though, the entire crowd sat in the field in front of Jesus. Mary smiled to herself at the look on the disciples' faces. They were panicked. If food didn't show up from somewhere, Jesus might lose all these followers.

Mary wondered if she was the only one who expected a miracle.

Then Jesus took the food and looked up to heaven. "Thank You, Father, for providing. We give You thanks in all things. Amen."

He began to tear the fish apart and break the loaves into pieces, handing basketfuls of the bread to the disciples. But with each break the bread and fish multiplied. Right before their eyes. Mary and Mary Magdalene, along with many of Jesus's longtime followers, watched in awe from the background as men, women, and children ate their fill.

When the meal was over, the disciples picked up twelve baskets of leftover pieces. Mary could hear them quickly calculate how many people ate from the five loaves and two fish that day. The estimate showed the extent of the miracle: five thousand men, and too many women and children to count.

Again Mary wished Joseph were alive. How proud he would've been to see the miracles that came at the hands of Jesus. The Messiah entrusted to their care had learned so much from His stepfather. Mary could see Joseph's impact in the way Jesus spoke calmly to the crowds, and the way Jesus had absolute peace when hope seemed lost. Those moments drove home the truth to Mary.

She would miss Joseph as long as she lived.

The memory faded. She would spend a lifetime grieving the loss of Joseph. But Jesus would not have that luxury with the loss of John the Baptist. Clearly there would be no time to grieve. After the miraculous feeding, Jesus's efforts and work on behalf of the people continued to increase. More healings, more miracles, more proof that He was the Messiah.

And no one could believe what happened next.

Mary shifted her position on the blanket so she could see Jesus better. Again the memory of recent weeks filled her heart. After Jesus had fed the masses, He ordered His disciples into the boat. "Go ahead of me," He told them, "to the other side of the Sea of Galilee." Then He turned to the crowd and sent them away. Only Mary and a small group of followers lingered, watching. As the crowd left, Jesus turned and began hiking up the nearest mountainside.

Mary understood. Jesus still hadn't had any real time to grieve the loss of John. Of course He needed to be alone, to pray. That's when Mary had set out with a group of people toward the hill country of Judea, to see Elizabeth. Now that she was back she knew what had happened in the meantime.

Jesus had stayed up on the mountain by Himself, and when evening came the boat with His disciples was already a long way from land. It was being pounded by the waves because the wind was blowing against it. So Jesus had done something that had the whole region talking.

He had walked on water.

Peter had told them what happened next. The disciples were in the boat and when they saw Jesus coming toward them they were terrified. They thought He was a ghost. But Jesus called out to them, "Be brave! It is I. Don't be afraid."

Peter had responded first. "Lord, if it is You, tell me to come to You on the water."

And Jesus had told him to come.

The events that followed would be talked about by the disciples and maybe all people for all time. Peter actually stepped out of the boat and walked on water. Peter, the fisherman! For a moment he had actually stood on the waves. But then . . . Peter took his eyes off Jesus. Apparently when he saw the wind-tossed waves, he was afraid and began to sink. "Lord! Save me!" he cried out.

Again Mary smiled when she pictured her son, standing calmly on top of the water. As Peter was starting to drown, Jesus had held out His hand and helped him. "Your faith is so small!" Jesus told Peter. "Why did you doubt Me?"

The way Peter told the story, as the two of them climbed back in the boat, the wind died down and the disciples all agreed that Jesus really was the Son of God. As if they needed more proof. They sailed across the lake to Gennesaret and when the people there recognized Jesus they sent a message all over the nearby countryside. People brought their sick to Jesus. They begged Him to let those who were ill just touch the edges of His clothes.

And all who believed Him were healed.

But something happened in the following days that worried Mary. Some Pharisees and teachers of the law came from Jerusalem to see Jesus. Right away they started questioning Him about matters of the law. Why His disciples didn't wash their hands before they ate. Why He healed the sick on the Sabbath, the day set aside for rest. His actions defied tradition and riled the religious leaders.

Next the Pharisees came looking for trouble. Mary wanted to warn Jesus. But again she could do nothing but watch from a distance with His other followers. As always, Jesus didn't need her help. He took on the religious leaders and Pharisees, looking straight at them. "And why don't you obey God's command? You would rather follow your own teachings!"

He quoted Scripture and finally told

them, "You pretenders! Isaiah was right when he prophesied about you. He said, 'These people honor me by what they say, but their hearts are far away from me. Their worship doesn't mean anything to me. They teach nothing but human rules.' "

His statement silenced the Pharisees and teachers. Clearly angry with Jesus, they moved to the back of the crowd. Jesus watched them go, then turned to the crowd and raised His voice: "Do everything they tell you . . . but don't do what they do."

He went on to tell the people what was clean and unclean, and how no one should follow a blind guide or both would fall into a pit. Mary could see the religious leaders getting more and more furious. They wouldn't tolerate being spoken against this way.

Something in Mary's heart told her these people meant Jesus harm, that they wouldn't have traveled to see Jesus except to try to catch Him in some kind of crime. She felt her heart race, her fingers turn cold. If only Joseph were here. He had always known what to do when Jesus was in danger.

But now . . . now Jesus was on His own.

Special memories flooded Mary's heart, things she had treasured and stored up from the early days when Jesus was a baby. Only

Joseph had understood what it was like for Mary back then, so young and forced to travel from Nazareth to Bethlehem in her final month of pregnancy. Joseph had stood by her through it all. He had steadied her on the donkey and held her hand while Jesus came into the world.

Mary felt a shiver run down her arms. She had taught Jesus how to walk. Now He walked on water. She had fed Him from a spoon. Now He fed thousands. Jesus belonged to the world, no question. Whatever happened in the days to come, God would sustain Jesus, and He would sustain her. Mary believed that.

She would just feel better if Joseph were here to go through it with her.

They moved on from that place, the way Jesus and His followers were always moving on. They went to Tyre and Sidon, and while they were there, a Canaanite woman came to Jesus, crying out, "Lord, Son of David, have mercy on me!"

The followers of Jesus gathered around, amazed. Canaanites didn't associate with Jews, not at all. Yet this woman was unafraid. As she reached Jesus, breathless, she explained her trouble: "My daughter is demon-possessed. She is suffering terribly!"

Jesus remained quiet, thoughtful. Some of the men pressed in closer. "Send her away, Jesus. She keeps crying out after us!"

Again Jesus looked at the woman, as if His attention was hers alone. "I was sent only to the lost sheep of Israel."

The woman seemed to understand what Jesus meant. That Canaanites were not the people He had come for. The woman knelt before Jesus. "Lord, help me!"

Jesus narrowed His kind eyes, and Mary watched His followers hold their breath. "It is not right to take the children's bread and toss it to their dogs."

"Yes, Lord." The woman reached toward Jesus. "But even the dogs eat the crumbs that fall from their master's table."

A smile stretched across Jesus's face. "Woman, you have great faith! Your request is granted."

Later that day Mary and the others heard word that the woman's daughter was healed that very hour. Again and again Jesus defied tradition and customs, sharing the love of God, the healing power with all who believed in Him.

Mary and the others followed Jesus around the Sea of Galilee and there He miraculously fed another enormous crowd, but then more Pharisees and Sadducees came to put Him to the test. Their intentions were obvious, and again Mary felt fear rise within her.

As the conversation got under way, the religious leaders gathered around Jesus. "You're the Son of God." Their tone mocked Jesus. A few of them laughed. "How about You show us a miracle from heaven? Any miracle will do. Fire from the sky or a healing or two. Something."

Jesus stared at them, knowing their hearts and intentions.

Mary felt her knees tremble. *God, give me peace. Give us all peace. And please give Jesus the words to use with these men. Thank You, Father.*

Finally Jesus spoke. He talked about the signs of weather. "You know the meaning of what you see in the sky. But you can't understand the signs of what is happening right now." He took a step closer, restraint tempering his voice. "An evil and unfaithful people look for a miraculous sign. But none will be given to them except the sign of Jonah."

The Pharisees raged at this and their plot to kill Jesus became public.

Many of the followers decided to head to Jerusalem rather than to Caesarea Philippi and Capernaum, where Jesus traveled next.

The Passover was coming, which meant Jesus and the disciples would eventually make their way to the temple, to Jerusalem.

Then they'd be at Jesus's side for whatever came next.

When they arrived in the city, Mary heard news that made her wonder if she'd been wrong about Jesus's fate. The religious leaders might not have liked Him, but the people were drawn to Him. They talked of His being a king and they looked forward to His return to the city.

After Mary had been in Jerusalem a few days, she met up with several of her sons, including James, who pulled her aside. "Mother, what are you doing? Traveling with Jesus's followers?" He looked around, obviously nervous that someone might be listening. "He thinks He's God!"

"James, listen to me." Mary put her hand on his shoulder. "Jesus is not a liar. You should know that."

"So you believe Him?"

"I know what I've seen." She smiled at him. "Besides, Jesus is my son. I will always support my sons. No matter what."

The color in James's face deepened. "Don't you see what's happening here?" Again he looked around. "The people want a king. Someone to overthrow Roman rule."

James's voice grew more intense. "They're expecting a man with a royal robe and a crown complete with a whole army. When Jesus returns here, if He doesn't bring down the Romans, the people will hate Him."

Mary hadn't thought about that. She nodded, wondering if James was right. "God is in control. I know that much."

"You must keep your distance." His concern shone in his eyes. "Otherwise they could harm you, too."

"You think they'll harm Jesus?" Mary looked around the temple courts. An anticipatory feeling of celebration filled the air. "Only the Pharisees and Sadducees have a problem with Him. The people love Him, James. I've seen it myself. They come from everywhere and He heals them."

"Fine." James clearly didn't believe her. "All I'm saying is we have to be careful."

"Mary," one of Jesus's followers approached her, "we're going to find food. Come with us."

She looked at James. "I have to go."

"I'll be here." James hugged her and then took a few steps back. "I'm staying with friends. When things get bad come find me."

"I'll be fine." Mary looked at her son for a long moment, willing him to understand, praying he might believe the way she did.

Then she turned and went with the other followers.

Days passed and finally it was a week before Passover. Word was that Jesus and His disciples had reached Bethphage on the Mount of Olives, and now they would be heading to Jerusalem. Mary rejoiced at the response of the people. Everywhere she went they were talking about Jesus, excited for His arrival. As the hour neared, tens of thousands of people lined both sides of the entrance to the city. Some spread their cloaks on the road, while others cut palm branches from the trees and laid them out.

Mary took her place along the road with Mary Magdalene and several of Jesus's most devout followers. "I was so worried before this week," Mary Magdalene admitted. "I thought they were going to harm Him."

"I think we all thought that." Mary reveled in her sense of relief. This show of support was what Jesus deserved, especially after He had healed and loved so many throughout the region. He was a king and He was worthy of this praise.

A commotion sounded in the distance along the road. Mary felt her heart leap. "It's Jesus . . . He's headed this way!"

As He came into view, Mary could see Jesus sitting on a donkey, His disciples walking beside and behind Him. All around her the people began to shout, "Hosanna to the Son of David! Blessed is He who comes in the name of the Lord!"

Mary closed her eyes and let the words wash over her soul. Yes, this was what Jesus had earned. After weeks of uneasiness and concern, after moments of all-out fear, Mary felt at peace. The people shouted the words over and over again.

Some people came running up to see what was happening. "Who is this?" they cried out.

In loud voices the crowd responded, "This is Jesus, the prophet from Nazareth in Galilee."

Like so many times in Jesus's life, Mary treasured the moment in her heart.

As Jesus reached the place where Mary stood in the crowd, He did what He often did when he was near her. He looked her way.

His look should've been confident and filled with joy. This was His hour. His kingdom was at hand! Instead, Mary saw a depth of pain that defied words. And in that instant she knew: Something was wrong. No matter how happy the people were, regardless of how welcoming their reception, trouble was stirring. She could see it in Jesus's eyes. That wasn't all. She could also see that He loved her, and He was concerned about her.

Of course He was concerned. He had promised Joseph He would care for her and now they'd been apart for several weeks. Mary nodded at Jesus, trying to convey the fact that she was fine. That her only worry was for Him. He understood, clearly. A slight smile eased the tension in His expression and He nodded at her.

Then the moment passed. Jesus and His disciples continued on the road toward the temple. All the while the people threw down their cloaks and tree branches so that the hooves of the donkey carrying Jesus never touched dirt. And they continued to shout praises and "Hosanna to the Son of David! Blessed is He who comes in the name of the Lord."

"Let's go to the temple." Mary Magdalene touched Mary's arm and nodded. "Lots of His followers are going there."

Mary agreed. She could hardly imagine how things could turn bad at this point, not with the whole city throwing a welcome party for Jesus. But there was no misreading the look she'd seen in Jesus's eyes.

Something terrible was coming.

■ ■ ■ ■

They made their way through the crowd to the temple just as Jesus was arriving there. Somehow the mood felt different, more tense. All eyes were on Jesus and gradually the crowds quieted. As if oblivious to the masses, He stared at the ring of vendors and money-changers.

Mary knew what Jesus was thinking. Vendors had no right setting up in the temple courts to sell doves and other items of sacrifice. People were supposed to bring their sacrifices from home. But since there was money to be made, the new law stated that those visiting the temple had to purchase their items here.

Usually at an inflated price.

The practice wasn't fair and it wasn't what was intended for Passover week. Suddenly Jesus rushed to the nearest table and flipped it over, scattering the vendor's doves and coins. A gasp came from the crowd and people stepped back, getting out of His way. Mary held her breath, watching as Jesus did the same thing to the other vendors' and money-changers' tables.

Then in a booming voice He shouted, "It is written: My house will be called a house of prayer, but you are making it a den of robbers!"

Many in the crowd clapped and cheered — those who before this moment had no choice but to pay the price for a sacrifice. But Mary could see clusters of Pharisees and Sadducees gathered in the corners, whispering among themselves. They were the ones who profited from this setup and all of them looked angry at what had just happened.

Finished with that task, Jesus moved to another section of the temple courts, and there He did what He was most comfortable doing: He began to teach and heal people. Mary wondered if James might be somewhere in the crowd, looking on and watching as blind people received sight and those without hearing heard sound for the first time.

Tears stung Mary's eyes as she watched from a distance, gripped by the scene. No matter how often Jesus had done this, the celebration never grew old. She smiled at the children shouting and dancing near Jesus. "Hosanna to the Son of David!" they cried out. "Hosanna to Jesus!"

At one point the chief priests and teachers of the law approached Jesus, scrutinizing Him as He continued healing the people.

They seemed particularly bothered by the voices of the children. Finally one of them shouted, "Do you hear what these children are saying?"

Jesus turned to the one who had spoken. "Yes. Have you never read, 'From the lips of children and infants You, Lord, have called forth Your praise'?"

Mary could see this angered the religious leaders, but they did nothing about it — not in the midst of the crowds of people lauding Jesus's arrival. Instead they scuttled into the shadows. When they were gone, Jesus waved off the people. "I must go. But I will be back."

On His way out of the temple courts, He came to Mary and hugged her. "Are you okay?"

"I am well, Jesus." She hesitated. "Just concerned for You."

He smiled. "I'll be fine. My Father is with Me." He looked beyond her to the temple gates. "I am going with My disciples to Bethany for the night. Walk with Me."

Mary could feel the eyes of the religious leaders on them as they left the temple courts. They took a less traveled road through the city. Somehow the crowds didn't seem to notice Him, and for the first time in months Mary and Jesus were sharing a private moment.

"I need to talk to you." Jesus slowed His pace. "Things are going to get bad very soon." He looked at her. "I wanted you to hear it from Me."

A rush of fear raced through Mary's veins, but she didn't look away, didn't waver. "You've said it a few times . . . to the followers. That the end was coming."

"Yes." Jesus looked straight ahead again. "The end of My earthly ministry will happen here." He was quiet for several steps. The street remained nearly empty, and up ahead was a bench in the shade of a large olive tree. "Let's sit there so we can talk."

Again Mary steeled herself for whatever was ahead. They took their seats beside each other and Mary turned so she could see Jesus clearly. She had missed moments like this. Before He left home, she and Jesus would talk often. He was always considerate of her needs, her feelings. But lately He'd been too busy for more than a quick glance or a passing comment.

"First, I want you to know something." Purpose rang in Jesus's voice. "I promised Joseph I would take care of you, and I will do so. Until My final breath. You'll never have to worry or want for anything, Mother."

"Jesus." Mary touched His cheek. "You've always been so considerate."

He smiled, though His eyes held a deep sadness. "You've been the best mother I could've had. I want you to know that." He searched her eyes. "You were chosen for this, and you've been faithful. When I was a child and now. Even though My brothers don't believe, you do."

"It hasn't always been easy. I've wavered, Jesus." She looked down at her lap. "That night . . . at the house in Nazareth." Her eyes lifted to His. "I'm sorry about that. I didn't want anyone to harm You."

"I know." He smiled, his eyes tender.

"Obviously, I've known the truth about You since the angel Gabriel's visit." She leaned against the bench. "And now, after what I've seen, of course I believe. You are the Messiah, Jesus."

"Yes." A heaviness came over Him. "But I'm also your son. And that's why I have to tell you what's about to happen."

If Mary could've found a way to stop time, she would have. Then she and Jesus could sit here on this bench in the shade of this olive tree and talk for hours. Or forever, even. Instead, she sensed time rushing ahead, and she couldn't do anything to stop it. She nodded, too afraid to speak.

Jesus took hold of Mary's hand. "I've been telling My disciples this. I even told them on the way into the city the other day." He paused. "Now I need to tell you."

Mary could barely breathe. If only Joseph were here to share this moment. *God, give me strength . . . I can't do this on my own.* She struggled to speak. "Go ahead, my son."

He watched her for a while, as if waiting until He was sure she could take the impact of what He was about to say. "In the days to come I will be delivered over to the chief priests and the teachers of the law."

An ache started at the center of Mary's heart. "Jesus . . ."

"There's more." He leaned closer, looking intently into her eyes. "They will condemn Me to death and hand Me over to the Gentiles to be mocked and flogged . . ." Jesus hesitated. "And to be crucified."

Mary closed her eyes and shook her head. The grief coursing through her body was almost more than she could bear. This couldn't be happening. Jesus was loved by the masses. They wouldn't tolerate seeing Him crucified. She wanted the conversation to be nothing but a bad dream, but that was impossible. Jesus's hand was still holding tightly to her own. When she opened her eyes He was looking straight at her. "Why, Jesus?"

"These things must happen to fulfill the prophecies about Me." Peace emanated from Jesus's kind eyes. "Mother, it must be this way. I wanted you to hear it from Me."

"But they love You." Tears welled up in Mary's eyes. "They'll never harm You."

Jesus drew a long breath and looked back toward the temple. "They love Me today. But not for long."

"So they'll mock You and beat You and crucify You? What about Your followers, Jesus?"

"As I told John's disciple that day, blessed is the man who doesn't lose faith on account of Me." Jesus turned to Mary again. "There's more."

Mary wasn't sure what else there could be. The news was devastating already.

"On the third day, I will be raised to life." A certainty filled Jesus's tone. "Don't you see, Mother? I will conquer death for all time. For everyone who believes in Me."

The idea was more than Mary could understand. She figured Jesus meant that He'd go to heaven. That He would live again there. "But it will be the end of Your life here."

"Yes. It is time for Me to go be with My

Father." He smiled at her, His head angled as if He were willing her to be at peace with all of this. "There I will prepare a place for you, Mother. And for all those who follow Me."

Mary nodded. For a while neither of them said anything. Images ran through Mary's heart and mind, moments from Jesus's childhood. "You were the sweetest baby."

He smiled. "I remember how worried you were that Passover when I was twelve."

"Hmmm." Mary felt a sad sort of smile lift the corners of her mouth. "You could've told us You were teaching."

"It just sort of happened. I understood in that moment I was doing what I was born to do." He smiled. "I figured you would know that."

"Yes." Mary uttered a quiet laugh. "We should've known. I agree."

Mary thought about all she'd carried with her lately. "I'm sorry about James and the others. They still . . . they don't believe."

"I know." Jesus's tone held not a hint of anger. "They will in time."

That one bit of good news gave Mary hope for what was ahead. "I believe that." She smiled. "I really do."

Again they looked at each other, neither wanting the moment to end. Mary thought about all that was to come, the way wicked men would arrest and harm Jesus and eventually kill Him. "I will stay by You till the end, Son." Her voice cracked under the weight of her hurting heart.

"Thank you." Jesus leaned in and hugged her, the way He had done when He was a boy. The way He might never do again. "I love you."

Tears slid down Mary's cheeks. "I love You, too."

"I need to go. My disciples are waiting." Jesus helped Mary to her feet. One last time He looked straight through her, to the place in her heart where she would always be His mother. "I want you to remember this moment. Remember I told you these things would happen." He hesitated. "They have to take place. It's God's will, Mother." He took both her hands. "Okay?"

She wanted to scream that none of this was okay. "There's no other way?"

Jesus shook His head. "None." He released her hands and gently wiped one of her tears with His fingertip. "Mother, will you remember?"

Mary nodded. "I will."

"Okay." Jesus took a few steps back. He pointed behind them down the street where they had come from. Mary Magdalene and the others are waiting for you." He smiled at her. "See you tomorrow. In the temple courts."

Mary waved and watched while He walked away. Then she turned and walked back to the others. How could she stand up under all that would happen in the days to come? She thought about Elizabeth's words. *You get up in the morning. You take one step and then another. Somehow you learn to inhale again.* She could do nothing to stop her tears as she reached the others, but none of them seemed to notice. Mary was glad. Long ago, she had needed time to ponder the birth of her son.

Now she would need time to ponder His death.

Trouble started for Jesus as soon as He showed up at the temple courts the next morning. Mary was there, tired from a mostly sleepless night. When she arrived, Mary Magdalene had asked her what was wrong but she didn't go into detail. "Things are about to get bad for Jesus. I need to be ready."

Mary Magdalene ____ ed to understand. Now they were sta____ ____ together, waiting as Jesus returned. ____ of people had gathered, and Jesus ____ voice filled with kindness and compassion. He told of a fig tree He had seen on the way back into the city. And He taught about the importance of praying in faith. As He was talking, something caught Mary's attention.

The chief priests and elders had formed a group and now they were approaching Jesus even as He taught. One of them stepped forward and shouted, "By what authority are You doing these things?" The man pointed. "And who gave You this authority?"

Jesus turned and studied them for several seconds. "I will also ask you one question. If you answer Me, I will tell you by what authority I am doing these things." He moved a few steps closer to the religious leaders. The crowd watched, breathless. "John's baptism: where did it come from? Was it from heaven, or of human origin?"

Mary wasn't sure whether to cry about the fact that John was still so heavy on Jesus's heart, or cheer out loud because He was so brilliant. Like the others with her, she chose to simply watch and wait. All eyes were on the religious leaders now. They looked at Jesus and then at each other. After a few seconds they huddled together. Occasionally one of them would turn around and look from Jesus to the growing crowd.

Then they'd huddle again.

Jesus's followers whispered among themselves. "He has them in a bind," one of them said. "They all know John was a prophet. They believe that. If these men say John's baptism was from heaven — as it was — then they will also have to believe what John said about Jesus. But if they say 'from human origin,' the people will rise up against them."

Finally the men turned and faced Jesus again. "We don't know."

A chorus of snickers rose from the crowd. The chief priests and the elders of the people didn't know. And that could only mean one thing: Jesus knew more than they did. Mary savored the victory, as again all eyes turned to Jesus for His response.

He shrugged, letting the cowardice of their answer sink in. "Neither will I tell you by what authority I am doing these things."

The crowd burst out in applause, cheering Jesus for outwitting the religious leaders. It was a high moment, one His followers relished. Mary watched her son, how He handled it. He didn't stand on a box and bow to the crowds or mock the religious leaders. He simply resumed His teaching.

For the next few days Jesus taught the crowd in parables, using the power of story to open their hearts and minds to the truth of the gospel. With the religious leaders hanging at the back of the crowd, scrutinizing Him, Jesus told a story about a man with two sons, only one of whom did his father's will. Mary would never forget what Jesus said that day, and the way He once more defended John.

"Truly I tell you, the tax collectors and the prostitutes are entering the kingdom of God ahead of you." He looked straight at the elders and chief priests. "For John came to show you the way of righteousness, and you did not believe him, but the tax collectors and the prostitutes did believe. And even after you saw this, you did not repent."

The Pharisees and chief priests knew Jesus was talking about them, and the crowd knew they were looking for ways to arrest Jesus. But clearly the religious leaders were outnumbered, and so Mary watched them wait. As they did, Jesus's condemnation of religious legalism and stubborn pride continued story after story.

Jesus talked about how the kingdom of God would be taken away from some and given to people who would produce fruit, and He spoke of having the right wedding clothes or otherwise being thrown out of the eternal banquet. Even now Mary wished

Joseph could see the way He faced His fate without fear.

Warning after warning. Jesus continued to teach the people. Always He had an eye on the dark corners of the temple courts, where the religious leaders plotted against Him.

Mary did as she had promised her son: she stayed close enough that she could hear what was happening, close enough to watch the drama play out. Again the Pharisees and Sadducees tried to trick Jesus with questions about taxes and marriage at the resurrection. Jesus answered with godly wisdom each time, and most often the religious leaders walked away scratching their heads, amazed at His teaching.

With the Sadducees unable to find a way to bring Jesus down publicly, the Pharisees got together. One of them, an expert in religious matters, tested Him with this question: "Teacher, which is the greatest commandment in the Law?"

Mary loved the look on Jesus's face as He turned to the man. It was the sort of look a loving parent might give a troubled child. Stern but patient. And not the least bit perplexed. Mary narrowed her eyes, watching her son. *Give Him the right words, Father . . . Be with Jesus.* How could she stand by and watch anyone hurt Him?

Jesus raised His voice, no doubt so the crowd could hear His answer. "Love the Lord your God with all your heart and with all your soul and with all your mind. This is the first and greatest commandment." He paused, unwavering in His attention to the man who asked. "And the second is like it: 'Love your neighbor as yourself.' " He looked around at the crowd. "All the Law and the Prophets hang on these two commandments."

The crowd started to applaud again, but Jesus held up His hand. He took a few steps toward the group of Pharisees. "What do you think about the Messiah? Whose son is He?"

One of the men lifted his face, prideful and arrogant. "The son of David," he said. He nodded at his peers and they did the same, clearly agreeing with the response.

Jesus waited until the courtyard was quiet again. "How is it then that David, speaking by the Spirit, calls Him 'Lord'? For he says, 'The Lord said to my Lord: "Sit at my right hand until I put your enemies under your feet." ' "

The Pharisees blinked a few times, silenced again.

"If, then," Jesus continued, "David calls Him 'Lord,' how can He be his son?"

Silence hung over the temple courts. Again Mary could've shouted for joy. Jesus was so much smarter than the Pharisees or Sadducees or the high priests. He was God in the flesh and He proved it day after day, answer after answer. She watched the Pharisees, their expressions tightly knit in anger. One of them opened his mouth to say something, but then he seemed to change his mind. After a minute or so, they pulled together in a group and left the temple courts.

It was the last time any of the religious leaders dared ask Jesus another question in public. Some of the followers thought this was a good sign. Jesus had escaped the scrutiny of the elders. But Mary knew different. Now the plans against her son were simply happening in private. Which could only mean one thing.

Jesus's day of reckoning was drawing near.

One afternoon a few days before Passover greater crowds gathered than at any other time that week. Jesus spoke about the Pharisees and teachers of the law. Rather than a teaching, this time His words were more of a proclamation. Seven times He started His statements against the religious leaders by saying, "Woe to you . . ."

He called them hypocrites, men who shut the door of the kingdom of heaven in people's faces. "You yourselves do not enter, nor will you let those enter who are trying to." He also called them children of hell and blind guides, greedy and self-indulgent, full of wickedness and dead men's bones. "You snakes! You brood of vipers! How will you escape being condemned to hell?"

With each passing indictment, Mary cringed. Jesus was right, of course. But any moment she expected guards to rush over and arrest Him. He could speak against the religious leaders only so long before something bad would happen to Him. After all, Jesus had told her Himself that it was coming. Mary wanted to cover her face and watch through the cracks of her fingers.

All she could do was pray and wait.

Finally it was the night of the Passover. Word on the street was that Jesus planned to share the Passover meal with His disciples somewhere in the city. But something must have gone terribly wrong, for late that night she heard shouting and screaming in the streets, people running through Jerusalem with the news.

Jesus had been arrested.

Mary rushed to get dressed, her heart racing, then she hurried into the street to meet

Mary Magdalene and the other followers. The details of what happened were revealed in the wee hours of the night. Apparently Judas Iscariot — one of Jesus's twelve disciples — had betrayed Him to the chief priests, sold Him for thirty pieces of silver.

Before Jesus was arrested, one of His disciples drew out a sword and cut off the ear of one of the armed men. Jesus's response was being repeated throughout Jerusalem that night, bringing comfort to His followers. Jesus had ordered His disciple to put away his sword. "Do you think I cannot call on My Father, and He will at once put at My disposal more than twelve legions of angels? But how then would the Scriptures be fulfilled that say it must happen this way?"

Then — as if things weren't bad enough — as the armed men led Jesus away, His disciples deserted Him. Every single one of them fled the scene. Even Peter. Mary wept when she heard the news. These were Jesus's closest friends. The ones who had been present for every miracle and healing. Jesus had told them this would happen, but they must've had some other outcome in mind.

Now Jesus was in the hands of Caiaphas, the high priest, imprisoned in the place where the teachers of the law and the elders assembled. Mary and Mary Magdalene, along with many of Jesus's followers, went to that place and kept watch in the courts. The minutes became hours and Mary couldn't take her eyes off the gates of the place where Jesus was being kept.

Sometime in the early morning James found her. "I'm so sorry, Mother." He framed her face with his hands. "I'm here for you. Whatever happens."

The gates didn't open until later in the morning, when several chief priests and elders led Jesus out and handed Him over to Pilate, the governor. Mary watched the strength in Jesus's shoulders, the kindness and determination in His eyes. She knew her son. He was not afraid of what they were going to do to Him. Even so, Mary wanted to run through the crowd and push the men away, grab Jesus by the hand the way she had when He was a little boy, and take Him somewhere safe.

"You can't go to Him," James whispered to her.

She nodded, never taking her eyes off Jesus. "I know."

"I'm sorry." James stood straight at her side. "But they would only hurt you, too."

Mary would explain it all to James later.

For now she kept her attention on Jesus. Once He was in Pilate's keeping, the crowd moved outside the governor's gates. They were there when Mary first heard the news about Judas. People were shouting and crying out, so Mary had to lean in to understand what they were saying.

Apparently after Jesus had been condemned, Judas was seized with remorse. He tried to return the thirty pieces of silver. But it was too late. The high priests would do nothing to change Jesus's fate. Desperate and unwilling to face Jesus again, Judas threw the money into the temple and went and hanged himself.

Mary reeled from the news. Yes, she knew what was coming. But the response of Jesus's disciples was shocking. Sometime that morning James spoke up again. "Mother, you should leave this place. It isn't safe."

"No, James. I want to be here."

"People are very upset. If the crowd turns on Jesus, they'll turn on you."

Mary watched her son and her heart hurt for him. "You still think Jesus is crazy." She breathed in, steadying herself. "You will see soon enough, James." She faced the governor's gates once more. "As for me, I will remain at His side. I promised Him that."

The crowd around them was growing. The chief priests and elders knew about Pilate's custom of releasing a single prisoner, so they infiltrated the people, disparaging the name of Jesus and inciting them to turn against Him. "You wanted a king, right?" they shouted at the people. "Someone to overthrow the Roman rule and free the Jews!" Then they would point at the governor's gates. "Look there. You must have the wrong man. Jesus isn't a king. He's not going to overthrow anyone."

As they worked their way through the masses, their words hit their mark. The people began to grumble among themselves, questioning whether they should've supported Jesus after all. Then the chief priests took it a step further: "Jesus is a liar. He lied to you on purpose to trick you. If Pilate lets us release a prisoner, choose Barabbas. Jesus should be killed for lying to you!"

Mary wanted to find a place high above the crowd and scream at them. How could they forget so quickly the countless people Jesus had healed? Why would they turn against the One whose teachings had stumped the Pharisees and Sadducees? Hadn't they seen one miracle after another? But now in a matter of hours the religious leaders were swaying the people away from Him.

Just as His own disciples had been tricked into abandoning Him.

Mary cried silently, refusing to be comforted by James or Mary Magdalene or any of the others. She had prepared herself for the physical pain Jesus was about to endure. But she had never imagined what it would feel like to see Him betrayed. Just a week ago the people were throwing their cloaks down as He entered Jerusalem.

Now, one by one, they were turning against Him.

As the noon hour drew near, Pilate did indeed appear to the people. "Which of the two do you want me to release to you?" he asked the crowd. "Jesus or Barabbas?"

With terrifying certainty, as if their answer had been rehearsed, the people shouted, "Barabbas!"

Mary's heart sank. The religious leaders had accomplished what they set out to do. Even Pilate seemed surprised. Mary squinted against the midday sun, watching his reaction. He blinked a few times and then moved to the edge of his balcony. He raised his voice to the people: "What shall I do, then, with Jesus who is called the Messiah?"

The crowd shouted even louder than before. "Take Him away! Crucify Him!"

Mary gasped and her hand flew to her mouth. "No," she muttered. She turned to James and then Mary Magdalene. Never mind that Jesus had told her this would happen. The reality was too much to bear. She grabbed the sleeve of James's garment. "Why are they saying that? They can't mean it."

James put his arm around her and the other Mary leaned in close. Wherever Jesus was, if He could hear the crowd He had to be crushed. The same people who had cried out "Hosanna!" were now calling for His death! Mary felt sick to her stomach. But she didn't cry or fight with the people around her. No matter how horrible things were, she had to keep telling herself: this was God's plan.

Again Pilate looked stunned. "Shall I crucify your king?"

"We have no king but Caesar!" the chief priests and the people yelled in response.

Mary stared at the people. They had no idea what they were saying. Worse, she was sure they would get their wish. For generations and generations to come, the offspring of these people would have the blood of Jesus on them.

The thought was horrifying.

So Pilate released Barabbas to the people, and he announced that Jesus would be flogged and crucified. Mary's whole world was falling apart. She wanted to run and hide, ride out the rest of the traumatic day somewhere alone, in peace and quiet. Maybe up on the Mount of Olives. But she had to stay. She had to be there until the end.

She had promised Jesus.

The procession toward the crucifixion had begun.

Mary moved along the road through the crowd, keeping pace with Him. But her heart was back in Nazareth, back when Jesus was a boy and Joseph wouldn't have let anyone harm Him. The sights and sounds along the way were surreal, like something from the most terrible nightmare. But this wasn't a dream. The people were getting what they wanted.

Jesus was going to be crucified.

When Mary could bring herself to look at Jesus, every cell in her body hurt for Him. The skin on His back hung in bloody shreds and a crown of thorns had been pushed into His scalp. Despite His broken body and the loss of blood and fluids, the soldiers forced

Him to carry His cross. Several times when Mary caught a glimpse of Jesus, she had to pray to keep from fainting.

With everything in her she wanted only to take Him from this place, clean His wounds, and tend to His battered body. Several others walked along with her, followers who had not abandoned Jesus. They cried out and wailed at what was happening to Him.

But only Mary was His mother.

Halfway to Golgotha — the place where they would crucify Him — Jesus stumbled, the weight of the cross too much for Him to bear. "Jesus!" Mary cried, and with her remaining strength she pressed into the crowd, trying to close the distance between them. She took only three steps before somehow in the chaos, someone tripped her.

Mary landed facedown, the wind jolted from her lungs. She clawed at the dirt, the small rocks and gravel cutting into her hands and knees. *Breathe,* she ordered herself. *Take a breath!* She couldn't lie here on the ground. Jesus needed her. She stayed still, hunched over her knees, despite the crowd moving past her.

While she was still there in the dirt, a man snarled at her, "You can't save Him. Let Him save Himself." He sneered. "Stay in your place, woman!"

Gradually Mary grabbed a few quick breaths, then a few more. James was at her side, helping her up. "Mother!" He brushed the dirt tenderly from her scraped cheeks. "We have to get out of here now! Before something worse happens."

"I need to be with Him, James. Please . . . help me find a way to Him. He's the Messiah, no matter what anyone says."

James froze in place. "What?"

Even in the noise of the crowd, his mother spoke loud enough to be heard: "He is the Messiah. I've known that since before He was born."

"You've believed Him all along."

"Yes." His mother didn't break eye contact. "Even when I wanted to bring Him home to protect Him, I believed."

One of Jesus's followers, John, put his hand on Mary's shoulder. "We need to get to the road. Come on, Mary."

She nodded but kept her attention on James. "Are you coming?"

"No." He had to draw the line somewhere. "I am not one of His followers."

Mary could no longer talk around the issue or use gentle words with her son. She looked deep to his soul. "Jesus is the Savior. He is God in the flesh, James." She put her hand alongside his face. "He always has been."

The outrage and pain in James's expression said more than words ever could. He hesitated only a moment longer, and then he turned and pressed his way against the crowd. Mary watched him go, and then she brushed more gravel off her skirt and set off after Jesus.

She reached Mary Magdalene at about the same time she thought her first hopeful detail all day: the fact that John was here. He steadied her, his presence protective. He was Jesus's youngest disciple, the one Jesus had loved very much. Wherever John had disappeared to last night, he had come to his senses today. Now he stayed by Mary's side as they moved parallel to Jesus.

As they walked, John looked into her eyes. "I'm sorry. I never should've left."

"You're here now." Again Mary had to raise her voice to be heard above the chaos.

"I'll never leave again." John took hold of Mary's hand and stayed next to her as they moved forward. "Whatever the cost, I'll always be here."

John's presence gave Mary the strength she needed to go on. Strength to overcome her sorrow because of James's departure. Strength to overcome her grief over what was happening to Jesus. "God is here, Mary." John leaned close, his tone confident. "Everything will be okay in time."

They were words Mary needed to hear, but as they reached Golgotha, as Roman soldiers threw the cross on the ground and slammed Jesus down on top of it, Mary wondered if they would be enough. A soldier positioned the first nail near Jesus's right wrist. Another man took a heavy hammer and used his entire body to drive the stake straight through and into the wood.

Jesus's cry rose above the crowd, and for the first time the people grew quiet. It was happening. Jesus was being crucified. Mary's tears came in a flood of sorrow and anguish, the sobs tearing at her body. "Jesus!" she cried out. "Jesus . . . I'm here. I'm here, my son!"

Even as He writhed and shouted out in pain, the soldiers positioned the second stake, pressing it against Jesus's left wrist. Mary and John and Mary Magdalene were near Jesus, close enough to hear His labored breathing between cries.

This time as the soldier drove the stake through Jesus's wrist, Mary fell to her knees. "Jesus! No!" Her voice sounded almost unrecognizable, even to her. The guttural cry of a mother desperate to save her son.

John stooped down, his arm around her shoulders. "Mary, I'm here."

For a moment she tried to pull away from John, tried to push her way to the cross. They could kill her, too, for all she cared. As long as she could put herself between Jesus and the people hurting Him. But she gained only a few feet before one of the Roman guards shoved her back.

Once more John drew her close. "Remember His words, Mary. Please . . ."

His words . . . His words. Mary's sobs overtook her and she couldn't breathe, couldn't think. "Jesus!" Her voice was much fainter now, her strength nearly gone. Why were they hurting Him? He hadn't done anything but love people. And now the crowds gathered around wanting Him killed. Nothing made sense. She closed her eyes against the sight before her.

What were His words? She leaned against John, unable to do anything else. She pictured Him, her unbroken, unblemished son sitting beside her on the bench, holding her hand. Hadn't He said He would be crucified? Yes, that was it. He would be crucified because that had to happen to fulfill the Scriptures.

Her breathing came in rapid gasps. She would've done anything to block out the sounds around her, but she opened her eyes just as another stake was being driven through Jesus's feet. His cry rang across the area, again silencing the crowd. Mary closed her eyes again. She could hear the nails being driven into the wood. But this time they were nails being driven by Joseph in the carpenter's shop when Jesus was a boy.

The happy sound of her family working together.

Where was Joseph? Mary buried her head in John's shoulder. She had loved that man so much. Why wasn't he here to help her through this? To fight off the guards and rescue Jesus the way he had so many times before. *God, I need him. I need Joseph. Why are You letting this happen?*

She knew the answer. Knew it deep in her soul. The Scriptures needed to be fulfilled. But her mind and body were frantic with grief and all she could think was the obvious: she wanted the man she loved to rescue their son one last time. Needed to feel Joseph's arms strong around her the way they had been back when the two of them first started out.

"Mary." John was still beside her. "I won't leave you."

Yes, at least John was here. The disciple who had loved Jesus most of all. The only one who had returned for Jesus in this, His darkest hour. Joseph had been gone for many years, but here, during her most devastating minutes of existence, God still loved her.

She knew because He had given her John.

Mary leaned into John again and opened her eyes in time to see the soldiers raise the cross. A sign had been fixed to the top of it: *Jesus of Nazareth, the King of the Jews.* As the cross was raised, the weight of Jesus's body pressed against the stakes and He cried out again. He no longer had any leverage, any way to draw a breath without pushing against the stake in His feet, without scraping His bloodied back against the splintered wood of the cross.

"I can't stand this." Mary turned her face again into John's shoulder.

He must not have had any answers, because he said nothing. They were destroying Jesus, killing her son, and Mary could do nothing to stop them. But she could at least look His way. How else would she know if He needed her? She forced herself to turn and look at Jesus. Two thieves had been nailed to crosses on either side of Him. But Mary didn't even glance at them.

She couldn't look anywhere but at her

firstborn.

Around them the crowd grew loud again, hurling insults. "Come down from the cross if You are the Son of God!" one man yelled.

Mary tried to block out the voices. She looked past the blood-streaked, anguished face to her son's eyes. "Jesus . . ." Her voice was no more than a whisper.

The shouting around them continued, but somehow Jesus must've heard her. Because He turned His eyes to her and her alone. No words came from His bloodied mouth, but His look said everything Mary needed. The same eyes that had looked at her on the bench beneath the olive tree the other day. *God was still in control.*

Someone dipped a sponge in gall and held it up to Him. But after tasting it, He refused to drink. All the while the people shouted at Him, "He saved others but He can't save Himself!"

Mary shook her head. "No!" But again her voice was too weak to be heard. She was barely conscious, barely able to stand up under this. How dare they taunt Jesus? What had He ever done to them? Couldn't they see He was suffering? Mary held out both arms toward Him. "Jesus . . . I'm sorry."

Still the mocking continued. "He trusts

258

God. Let God rescue Him now!"

Suddenly one of the thieves called out to Jesus, "Remember me when You come into Your kingdom!"

Mary looked at the man and the slightest flicker of hope danced in the darkness of the moment. One more soul had believed Jesus. Even here at His worst moment. Jesus turned to the man, and though every word took effort He spoke loud enough for the crowd to hear, "Truly I tell you, today you will be with Me in paradise."

Paradise. Another spark of hope. The torture wouldn't last forever. Jesus was headed somewhere far better than this broken place. This place where people would crucify the Son of God.

Something caught Mary's eyes and she looked down. At the foot of the cross, Roman soldiers were casting lots for Jesus's clothing. As if this were all some sort of terrible game. "Stop!" she cried out. But they only laughed at her.

And for a single blessed moment Mary was a teenager again, wrapping Jesus in swaddling clothes, feeling the weight of her baby in her arms. She blinked and again she realized what was happening. They were gambling for Jesus's clothes! Suddenly she wanted to run at the soldiers and grab her son's garments from them. That much at least.

Instead it took all her remaining strength simply to breathe.

Jesus pressed His body upward and gasped for another breath. As He did, he shouted, "Father, forgive them, for they do not know what they are doing!"

When He finished speaking, darkness fell over the land — a darkness like no one had ever seen in the middle of the day. Mary looked up. Surely this would convince the people that they were crucifying the Messiah and not some imposter. They would see that this was the Son of God.

But they did not.

Around Mary the people were astonished at the darkness, but still they mocked her son, completely blind to the signs from heaven. In the midst of that moment, Jesus raised His voice again. "I am thirsty," He called out.

"Jesus!" Mary wanted to run to Him. When had there ever been a time that Jesus was thirsty and she hadn't helped Him? But she could only watch while the soldiers lifted wine vinegar to Him. Her breathing came faster, panic welling up within her. Jesus was suffering and she could do nothing about it.

Like every other time when Mary had felt on the brink of collapse, Jesus must've known. Because He turned to her one last time and His eyes shone with the deepest, most all-encompassing love Mary had ever felt.

A love she would carry with her forever.

Jesus pressed against the stake in His feet and drew enough breath to speak to her. "Woman" — His eyes lingered on hers and then shifted to John and back — "here is your son."

Mary clung to John, her tears overtaking her, clouding her vision.

Another press against the splintered wood and He spoke to John, "Here . . . is your mother."

The weight of Jesus's body fell against the nails, but Mary could see relief in His eyes. Then it hit her: this was His promise to her, His promise to Joseph. He would see that she was taken care of if it was the last thing He did.

Mary held her hand out toward Him.

Jesus's breathing was more and more difficult. With every labored breath, Mary could only watch like everyone else. It had been nearly three hours that Jesus had hung on the cross. The guards were breaking the legs of the thieves on the other two crosses.

Mary couldn't imagine watching them do that to Jesus.

One painful breath after another, Jesus fought for life. But something else was happening, something dark and excruciating. Mary could see the change in Jesus's face. In the midst of it Jesus cried out, "My God, My God, why have You forsaken Me?"

Some of those standing nearby mocked Him again. "Look at that! He's calling Elijah!"

Others said, "Let's see if Elijah comes to save Him!"

Mary couldn't stand another moment of seeing her son suffer. But she couldn't look away, either. She had promised Jesus she would be here till the end. In the midst of His agony, Jesus gasped for one final breath.

Then in a voice that was part tortured pain, part unspeakable peace, Jesus cried out again, "Father, into Your hands I commit My spirit." He hung His head and with what remained of His strength He said His final words: "It . . . is . . . finished."

"Jesus!" Mary reached out toward Him once more.

But it was over. Jesus no longer moved or tried to breathe. The son she had borne in a stable, the baby she had lifted up before wise men and kings . . . the child who had brought her nothing but love and joy was gone.

His suffering was finished. Mary wished only one thing as she turned away from the horror of Jesus's dead body on the cross: that — like the thief on the cross — she could be in paradise with Jesus today, too.

The guards came to break Jesus's legs, but He was already dead. One of them drew a sword and slashed at Jesus's side — as if to be sure. Mary gasped, horrified. At the same time the words of Simeon came rushing back. *And a sword will pierce your own soul, too . . .*

Simeon had known.

And now the prophecy had come true.

Before she could move or speak or begin to think about what to do next, the ground began to shake beneath her feet. All around Mary and John, people fell to their knees before the cross. And still the earth shook, more violently than before.

A screeching sound came from the dirt. Cracks began to split through the ground where the crowd now hovered on its knees before the dead body of Jesus on the cross. Nearby, tombs opened up and even in the darkness they could see the bodies of many holy people raised to life. Mary made a sound that was more laugh than cry. God was doing this. Just as Jesus had told her. This had to happen so the Scriptures would be fulfilled.

As the earthquake finally stopped, the centurion and those with him who were guarding Jesus at the cross cried out in voices filled with terror, "Surely, He was the Son of God!"

Vindication breathed life into Mary. Yes, He was the Son of God. Of course He was. Why it had taken this for the people to see? She wanted to shout at all of them for how terribly they'd treated Jesus, and how wrong they had been. But it was too late for that.

Too late to do anything but tend to Jesus's body. One last time.

Joseph of Arimathea came then and asked for Jesus's remains. When he had permission, Joseph and a few other men lowered the cross and removed the stakes. Mary was immediately at their side. She found water and a cloth and gently washed the dry blood from Jesus's face and arms. Someone brought a cloth to wrap His body, but Mary refused any help.

Instead she continued washing Him, cleaning Him. Her touch was gentle, as it had been years earlier when she had cared for the boy Jesus. Her tears helped wet His skin, and when she had cleaned Him, she took the cloth and wrapped her son, the way she had when He was an infant. It felt wonderful to do something, to help Him in some way. Then Jesus's followers carried His wrapped body to the tomb. The whole time Mary stayed at His side, right up until they placed Him in the cave. She had to be there beside Jesus.

Her last single act of love for her oldest son.

It was the third day, very early in the morning, and Mary was among those anxious to tend to Jesus's body. Since the death of her son, Mary had heeded Elizabeth's advice. She would get up each morning, take one step and then another, and somehow she was learning to breathe again.

The women walked in silence, each of them sobered by the task at hand. No one could hurt Jesus now. But if there was one thing Mary was going to do, it was take care of her son's body.

Their footsteps fell soft on the morning ground, the dew still fresh on the olive trees as they passed by. Most of the disciples had returned by now. They had gathered in an upper room not far from where Jesus lay buried in the tomb. They felt awful, of course. Defeated by their abandonment of

Jesus. Peter hadn't said a word or eaten a bite since his return.

Overall, the mood was dark and discouraging.

But still Mary had to go see to Jesus's body. The other women felt the same way. They kept walking until the tomb came into view. Mary squinted through the early morning light. "What . . ."

A few more steps and then the women stopped. They were mere feet from the tomb, but something had happened. The stone had been rolled away. "I don't understand." Mary took a step forward and then stopped. Her heart pounded and her breath caught in her throat. "What's happened?"

Suddenly two men appeared in front of them, their clothes gleaming like lightning. Terror ran through Mary, and she was the first to fall facedown to the ground in fear.

"Do not be afraid," one of the men said.

Do not be afraid? Wasn't that what . . . Suddenly Mary remembered the visit three decades ago. The men were angels! They had to be!

The other man spoke next. "Why do you look for the living among the dead?" He smiled. "He is not here. He has risen!"

The women rose to their feet. Mary's hand flew to her face and she gasped. Was this really . . . She couldn't finish her thought.

The first glowing man was talking again. "Remember how He told you, while He was still with you in Galilee: 'The Son of Man must be delivered over to the hands of sinners, be crucified and on the third day be raised again'?"

In a rush, everything Jesus had told Mary came back again. This was the third day! Of course! Why hadn't she remembered that part? The men disappeared and all that stood in front of them now was the empty tomb.

Mary and the others ran back to the room and told the men, who had to see the empty tomb for themselves. Over the next few days Jesus appeared to all of them — even Thomas, who had doubted more than the others.

More than that, He appeared to James! Mary thought about her conversation with Jesus. He had said that one day His brothers would believe, and now they did. James was determined to tell everyone about Jesus. He had told her he would serve Jesus the rest of his days.

Mary had no doubt.

Now, in the upper room, a satisfaction came over Mary's soul as she watched Jesus

hold out his nail-scarred wrists to Thomas.
Jesus was alive, but something was different. And finally Mary understood. Jesus had
been her son. But now He was far more:
her Lord.

Her risen Savior.

She left the upper room and walked by
herself for a ways, to a place where a field
opened up before her. Everything made
sense now. Joseph's determination to rescue
their son, Zechariah's song, and John the
Baptist's sacrifice. Elizabeth's heartache and
James's epiphany. Even Mary's great anguish at the cross.

All of it had led to this: Jesus's resurrection from the dead. Indeed He had con-
quered death for Himself and for all people
who would believe in Him. Mary lifted her
eyes to heaven and took a deep breath. The
air smelled sweet of spring. Jesus's work was
finished on the cross, but the cross hadn't
been the end of Jesus. He would live forevermore.

So that one day all those who believed in
Him would also live forevermore.

Mary still wished Joseph could've seen this
moment. He had been the love of her life,
her strength and supporter. Her best friend.
But one day she would see him again.
Because of Jesus. And she would look

forward to that until it came time for her to join him.

Every answer Mary ever wanted welled up inside her soul. As she turned to join the others in the upper room, something caught her eye. She looked back over her shoulder and what she saw out in the distant field made her smile.

Wild orchids.

WEEKLY APPLICATION AND GROUP DISCUSSION GUIDE: INTRODUCTION

Thanks for sticking with me through the storytelling. If you're like me, these stories have made you care about the family of Jesus, how their lives might have looked, and how their role in His story might have affected them. As you know, I wrote these stories anchored in Scripture, culture, and geographic relevancy. I connected the dots with storytelling — fiction. My way of bringing the Bible to life, helping us get to know the family of Jesus a little better.

Now it's time to take a closer look at the Bible.

The following pages include Scripture readings and questions for further reflection. You can work through the questions individually or in a group. If you're holding a book club or Bible study, the Group Discussion questions will help direct your discussion and guide your reading. The Group Discussion sections end with a

Homework question.

There are two subjects within *The Family of Jesus* that need addressing:

1. Locusts: Biblical scholars differ on whether the locusts eaten by John the Baptist were beans from the locust tree — or grasshopper-like insects. I found plenty of research to support either point of view. So for the purpose of this book — both the fictional pieces and the following Bible study pieces — I simply referred to his food as locusts. That way you can read it however you best imagine John's food to be.

2. Zechariah and Elizabeth's relationship to Jesus: Many biblical scholars consider Elizabeth and Mary to be related — but not specifically as cousins. Still, since Scripture says they were cousins, I went with that in fiction and in the Bible study. The relationship between Zechariah and Elizabeth and Jesus is not quite as clear in Scripture. We might think of Jesus as a second cousin or a cousin once removed to Zechariah and Elizabeth. We might think Jesus was technically related only to Eliz-

abeth — because His mother was Elizabeth's cousin. However we view it, this much is agreed on by most biblical scholars: Jewish culture in biblical times defined family relations somewhat differently than we do today in Western culture. A number of biblical scholars believe Zechariah and Elizabeth to be the aunt and uncle of Jesus. I went with that relationship, because it's a connection we understand. I liked it the most. And since I wrote these stories anchored in Scripture and rounded out with fiction, my choice is simply that. Mine. Please feel free to keep your own thoughts on exactly how Jesus was related to Zechariah and Elizabeth.

STUDY 1
JOSEPH
THE PROTECTIVE STEPFATHER

DAY 1
Read Matthew 1:18–19

Joseph was a man of loyalty
and quiet trust.

Here's something you might not know about Joseph: The Bible doesn't include one recorded word by the man. Not one. The closest we get is that he obediently named his son Jesus, and he faithfully served Mary and Jesus and his family all his life.

But I like to think of one more character trait in regards to Joseph. I think he must've been deeply in love with Mary. They must have shared a special bond, right? Because when God chose Mary, He also chose Joseph to be the earthly father for Jesus. As a couple they must've had a very unique love to handle the constant pressures of raising the Messiah.

Of course, Joseph's trust in God was challenged throughout most of his life. One angel visit after another turned Joseph's normal life upside down. But always Joseph was willing. When God asked him to act and make decisions with very little information, Joseph said yes. He was faithful and loyal and willing. It couldn't have been easy for Joseph.

But one thing seems certain by his actions: He loved Mary with all his life.

- The Bible describes Joseph as someone who was in "right standing" with God. Who do you know who fits this description of a righteous man or woman? What is that person like?

_____

_____

- Read Matthew 1:19–20. Matthew records that Joseph did not act quickly but "considered" what must be done. In what must have seemed like a disastrous situation, do you think Joseph was hoping for answers? What does hope do for you?

_____

_____

• Joseph and Mary were misunderstood
  and eventually fugitives on the run
  from their government. Have you ever
  been misunderstood? Have you ever
  had to suffer for something you believed in? Describe what happened.

_____

_____

A man of faith, Joseph learned to wait for divine guidance.

Joseph cared deeply for his family. After Jesus's birth, Herod eventually died and an angel told Joseph it was time to leave Africa and head home. Joseph knew he was protecting a fugitive. Everywhere they traveled he was looking over his shoulder, wondering if someone was lurking close by, ready to attack his son.

Along with this ever-present threat, Joseph most likely burned through much of his savings while living in a foreign land. The carpenter shop, after all, was back in Nazareth. Can you imagine the questions he must have had? The temptation to worry?

Joseph must have wondered about provisions. He must've realized that other people, children no less, had been murdered on account of his son, the Prince of the world.

But still Joseph persevered. He cared for Mary and Jesus in complete obedience to God. No wonder God chose him to be the earthly father of Jesus.

- What is the recurring theme in these verses?

  _____

  _____

- Are you now, or have you ever been, in a season of uncertainty? How did you handle that time?

  _____

  _____

- Describe a situation when you responded patiently. What was the benefit?

  _____

  _____

Regardless of financial pressure, Joseph was faithful in following God's commands.

Joseph could never have been fully prepared for trying to protect and nurture the life of his stepson, the Savior of the world. He was righteous — right with God — and choosing to live that way equipped him with the capacity to love well.

Joseph became a devoted earthly father. It seems what little money they had, from Joseph's doing freelance carpentry work and from the gifts of the magi, was gone. So when Joseph followed the angel's prompting and returned his family to Nazareth, like most laborers he had to rebuild his business, reestablish his family. A lot was going on for Joseph. Still, regardless of the financial pressures and family needs, he never forgot that Jesus belonged to God, or the fact that Jesus was God.

Joseph and Mary were both careful to fulfill their duties under the law. When it was time to dedicate Jesus and consecrate Him to the Lord, they made the trek to

Jerusalem. Since they were not wealthy, they could not afford to sacrifice a large animal on Jesus's behalf. Instead they sacrificed two doves.

- Joseph was quick to trust and obey. Is it hard for you to trust? Whom do you trust the most? Why?

  _____

  _____

- Are there times when the pressure to meet the expectations of a boss or family members keeps you from being faithful to the ways of God? Explain.

  _____

  _____

- How could you keep God first even in uncertain times? Give an example.

  _____

  _____

God often writes our stories in ways we do not understand.

Jesus was growing up and both His earthly father and His heavenly Father were pouring character into Him. Sometimes we forget to see Joseph as a stepdad — meaning one who acts in place of an actual father. Being a stepparent is challenging. Joseph watched his oldest boy grow and mature. He taught Jesus his craft; they did carpentry work together. But even as he watched his son, even as he understood that Jesus was the Messiah, certainly much remained that Joseph didn't understand.

Remember the story when Jesus was twelve? That really happened. Mary, Joseph, and Jesus were on a family trip to Jerusalem when Jesus decided to stay in Jerusalem — and not tell anyone. The family thought He was coming along, as expected, but suddenly they discovered he wasn't actually with the caravan. He was missing for three days, until finally they found Him in the temple in Jerusalem having lessons with the rabbis.

When confronted with His behavior, adolescent Jesus stated what He clearly thought was the obvious: "Didn't you know I had to be in My Father's house?"

Poor Joseph. Even though he didn't understand his son, he had always been devoted to Him. Joseph probably even said to Jesus along the way, "What do you see?" or "What do you know?"

For Joseph this pondering would've been a day-by-day thing that continued in his heart from the time Jesus was born. I wonder if the lack of answers, the continual not knowing was what kept Joseph devoted. He was forced to trust in someone other than himself.

- Do you ever stop hoping, believing it would be less painful than to leave your heart open with desires that might never be met?

  _____

  _____

- Talk about a time when you didn't understand the people or situations around you. How was your relationship with God at that time? Explain.

_____

_____

Joseph consistently played out his role in
God's story.

What we gather from verse 23 is that Joseph spent his brief lifetime silently following Jesus. First following after Him as He toddled and learned to walk. And later following Him for salvation. The verse lets us know this: "He was the son, so it was thought, of Joseph." Those few words imply so much. Joseph clearly played the role of earthly father to Jesus. Why? Because everyone thought he was Jesus's actual father. That meant Joseph did all the things good fathers do — he led Jesus and taught Him and persevered as the leader of their family.

All of that, yet Jesus was never really his son. He was God's.

It becomes clear that Joseph and Mary treasured in their hearts what they knew about the destiny of their son. Joseph never deferred his responsibility as a stepfather, nor did he try to brag about who his son really was. "He was the son, so it was thought, of Joseph." Why? Joseph was quietly content to faithfully serve God by simply being a great dad.

- Can you think of a time, maybe when you were a child, when you longed to be something or become someone different from who you were?

  _____

  _____

- Explain the hope and joy that came when you figured out what you were actually created to do. If you haven't figured it out yet, how can you follow God's leading?

  _____

  _____

- What can the story of Joseph teach you about hope and perseverance?

  _____

  _____

For Group Discussion
What Can I Learn from Joseph?

> **Read 1 Corinthians 13:1–8**

Joseph's is a life that reflects
this kind of love.

1. Joseph patiently trusted God.

Joseph had no idea what was coming when
he agreed to stand by Mary. But it didn't
matter. He trusted God, regardless. The Life
Application Bible says, "The strength of
what we believe is measured by how much
we are willing to suffer for those beliefs."

A righteous man is often tested before he
is called. In our story, Joseph was tested
before he received his mission to love and
protect God in child form. Maybe you feel
as though God is leading you to a calling in
your life right now — you have a sense of
destiny. You may feel an anticipation welling
up in you. If you're on the brink of being
called, look around: a test of your values
and your convictions will probably precede
the clarity you long for.

Once you have a sense of how and where
God is directing you, are you willing to

move forward with incomplete information? Can you live in the tension of not knowing all the details right now? This is difficult, as we are all prone to maintain comfort, convenience, and control. Yet this is what keeps us devoted and pressing on in faith. Faith is learning how to keep moving in life in the absence of certainty. This kind of trust keeps us from leaning on our own understanding. Walking in faith causes us to look "unto Jesus the author and finisher of our faith" (Hebrews 12:2 KJV).

- Do you have a dream or sense of something that God is calling you to?

  _____

  _____

- Have your values been tested to show whether you can hold tightly to your convictions? Give an example.

  _____

  _____

2. Joseph was diligent and protective.

Joseph knew how to take care of the gift that had been entrusted to him. When we receive a gift, a child, a career, a dream come true, how do we hold it? Some of us hold tightly to whatever has been given to us. As a result, over time we often forget the blessing's origin.

Stewardship is always about holding something loosely. Remember the last time you were at the beach and you tried to hold sand in your hand? You gripped it, and what happened? It pushed out between your fingers and fell to the earth. But when you held it loosely, it stayed in the palm of your hand.

The same is true with our blessings. We stay diligent when we believe, "Every good and perfect gift is from above" (James 1:17).

- Joseph's task was caring for his wife and God's son. If you are a provider, what is it like to know that you are supposed to care for your family and protect them, yet at the same time look for cues from God?

_____

_____

- How do you find the balance between making the best choices you can and waiting for direction from God?

_____

_____

- If someone else provides for you, how do you feel knowing that you are cared for?

_____

_____

3. Joseph was content to serve behind the scenes.

Sometimes our role in the story is to blend into the background, quietly obeying. Listening. Sometimes we hesitate to do what is honorable in taking a lesser role because we are so deeply concerned with what people might think. We must be willing to serve often. For by doing so, like Joseph, we will love well and allow the credibility of our lives to spark a curiosity in those living without God.

My dad taught me to consider others more than myself. It's not an easy lesson. I remember when he attended one of my events a few years before he died. My reader friends had lined up for several hours to see me — something that always amazes me. My dad stood near me and leaned close. "Karen, remember this: There won't be autograph lines in heaven. This is just you making friends. One reader at a time."

I've held on to that truth ever since. I'm

nothing; God is everything. I tell stories for His glory. I meet with reader friends to deflect praise to the Lord. I seek to serve and love. So whether I'm at the front of the line or the back of the line, I can look at Joseph's quiet humility and find an example to live by.

What about you?

- What can you learn from Joseph about serving quietly, without fanfare?

  _____

  _____

- Have you ever had a background role in a given situation? How did that feel?

  _____

  _____

Homework: Joseph had to live his whole life knowing Jesus was the Messiah but not telling anyone. How good are you at keeping secrets? Determine as a group this week to refrain from gossip. When someone starts to share lurid details, you might say, "I'm focusing on the goodness in people this week. It's a challenge. Wanna join me?" When your group meets up again, be ready to talk about your experience.

STUDY 2
ZECHARIAH

THE KNOWING UNCLE

DAY 1
Read Luke 1:5–10 NIV

God blessed Zechariah and Elizabeth,
who were just ordinary people.

Zechariah and Elizabeth were fascinating to write about. The deepest desires of this godly couple's hearts simply had not been met. No matter how often they prayed or how deeply they believed, they never saw an angel or witnessed a miracle.

Most of all, they had no children.

You see, the very real Zechariah and Elizabeth were earthly travelers living in a routine, stuck on a small strip of land in the Middle East. In their culture, people regarded childlessness as a mark of divine displeasure, and so in a very personal way they lived daily under the burden of social disgrace. Regardless of the temptation to feel the shame of judgment, this couple chose to keep trusting — keep following God.

Then seemingly by chance Zechariah was invited into the Holy Place. There the incense burned and the smoke carried his requests to God.

Imagine standing in the Holy Place next to the altar alongside Zechariah, watching the smoke from the incense waft through the air and toward heaven. God received this as a sweet-smelling aroma, symbolic of the prayers of His people asking Him to save them and meet their needs.

On that day, in that place, God answered.

- Go back and read Luke 1:7. Have you ever felt as if your life was boring and lost in routine? Describe what that was like.

  _____

  _____

- Have you ever felt stuck, as though nothing was ever going to change? Describe it.

  _____

  _____

When our faith is shaky,
so is our worship.

Gabriel was an angelic being direct from the presence of God. As life-forms go, he was one of the most powerful beings in the universe. The experience of seeing him was so shocking that Zechariah's confidence seemed to drain from his body.

How about us? When we struggle with our faith, we find ourselves silent at times of worship. That's exactly what happened to Zechariah. In his case, he lived the next nine months in silence. No words. Imagine how hard that must have been for him: The confusion. The joy. The celebration. The story he was dying to tell, all bottled up inside.

He had to delay the telling of this story and, even more significantly, his song of praise. Even though Zechariah had a momentary faith lapse, God's blessing remained. He heard and granted the faithful man's requests. And eventually Zechariah was even able to praise!

- Have you ever had a moment when fear caused you to struggle in your faith?

_____

_____

- What is the difference between self-confidence and God-like faith?

_____

_____

- Have you ever had to go without speaking? What was that like?

_____

_____

As apprentices of Jesus, we are called to
walk in faith.

God meets people in movement. He longs
for His followers to walk in faith, especially
in the midst of confusion. He meets those
who come out to worship Him.

Just as Zechariah had in the years leading
up to the great announcement, he continued
to live by faith during his period of silence.
When tested by well-meaning but unin-
formed family and friends regarding the
naming of his son, Zechariah was quick to
reply with the written word: "His name is
John."

The desires of Zechariah's heart merged
perfectly with the desires of God's heart.
God blessed Zechariah's obedience and
gave back his voice.

- What does this statement mean: "God
  meets people in movement"? Give an
  example from your life.

_____

_____

- Can you remember a time when you felt God rewarded your earnest seeking?

_____

_____

When Zechariah received his voice back,
his first response was praise.

Finally Zechariah could speak! And the first
words from his mouth were not that he
finally had a son. Instead, he revealed that
he had been redeemed! His dominant desire
was to praise God for His salvation. And
how his very own son was going to prepare
the way for the Savior!

Zechariah had to have understood that
someday he himself would actually know —
through John — the Messiah. So when he
could finally speak, praise to God came first.
As much as he loved his son, Zechariah
displayed a greater longing to know his
Redeemer. All because he was faithful to
obey.

So ask. Ask for a job. Ask for financial
relief. Ask for a husband. A wife. Ask for
rescue from temptation. Ask for a son.

And in the waiting, enjoy conversation
with God.

Then when the answer comes, praise Him.
Of all the gifts you will ask for, He has

already given you His greatest: redemption. In the words of Zechariah, "Praise be to the Lord!"

- Why do you think God does not allow us to determine our own timetable for what we want to receive from Him?

  _____

  _____

- If you were unable to speak for nine months, what would you want to say first?

  _____

  _____

- Had God answered Zechariah's prayer for a son earlier in his life, he might have missed out, timewise, on giving birth to the forerunner of the Messiah. Looking back, share a time when you are glad God did not answer your prayer the way you first hoped.

  _____

  _____

Amidst the praise, Zechariah understood
his place in the story of God.

The birth of John made the story of God,
the story of redemption for His people, very
personal for Zechariah. His song of praise
gives us a window into that. He would be
the father of a son with a very specific mission.

Zechariah knew he must train his child in
such a way that his son understood that
God had set him apart. There was a design
upon John's life, and that design was
grander than any father could wish for his
son. Life would be different now. Things
would change. And John would be the
herald of that change.

God was breaking the silence. Jesus was
coming to the earth. John would prepare
the way. The prophet would precede the
Messiah. God was bringing the spiritual
deliverance that He had promised for so
long. Redemption was at hand!

Not only that, but Jewish culture of the
day defined family connections a little dif-

ferently than we do today. So because Mary and Elizabeth were cousins, Zechariah and Elizabeth would most likely be the uncle and aunt of the Messiah.

And Zechariah could see his role in the story!

- You also play a role in the story of God. How would you describe your role in that ongoing, eternal story? Do you have a glimpse of what God is doing through you? Explain.

  _____

  _____

- Can you recall a time when you kept living in faith, against all odds, and seemingly out of the blue God suddenly responded? How did you react? How did it feel to have clarity in that part of your story?

  _____

  _____

Read Luke 1:67–79

Zechariah was a man of worship.

1. Prayer makes us close to God and His will.

Zechariah prayed even without any sign of an answer. But the key here is that through constant prayer, Zechariah became very close to God.

We can be like that: we can pray to God about something and see no answer. Not for a very long time. Is it possible that in the asking you may actually grow closer to God? Oftentimes the answer is yes.

Jesus taught that God wants to be drawn into our lives through prayer. He is compelled when we ask!

- How do you respond when strangers ask something of you? What about family and friends?

  _____

  _____

- Do you think God enjoys being asked? Why? What keeps you from asking more of Him?

  _____

  _____

2. In the asking you gain a knowing.

As you ask things of God, you begin to know what God is concerned about, what He is like. God is always just and perfect and good. He gives provision. He knows what is best for us and what's required for His love story to move forward. His answers and direction come to us not according to our timetable but according to His. At just the right moment.

And when that moment occurs, we should have an overwhelming and immediate response — the same as that of Zechariah. Our mouths should form words of gratitude and praise.

- God knows you perfectly. Does that fact bring you comfort or concern? Why?

_____

_____

- What have you prayed about without seeing the response you're looking for?

_____

_____

- Is it possible to choose the truth over your feelings? Give an example of a time when you or someone you know was able to do this. How was it possible?

_____

_____

3. Believe in God's faithfulness.

Zechariah believed in God's faithfulness. Faith implies movement. Faith exposes us. We are creatures of comfort. By our nature we take the path of least resistance. Every time we believe in God, we choose *not* to place our faith in some false sense of security. Belief in God makes us give up any sense of control.

Zechariah understood this. He willingly

gave up control of his own dreams when, every day, he returned to God in prayer, believing. This is an important principle to understand when it comes to the tension of understanding God's will and our desires: if God has initiated the desire, He will answer the prayer.

Just be prepared.

The kingdom version of that answer may not look like the world's answer. Zechariah could never have imagined that his precious John — the one who would prepare the way for the Messiah — would be murdered as a young man. But God assured Zechariah early on, in Zechariah's song of praise, that there would be comfort in death.

Remember, this is just earth.

God wants us to be focused on eternity and helping others find Him along the way.

- Do you think the word *faith* implies movement? Give an example.

  _____

  _____

- When has something new or different exposed your insecurity?

  _____

  _____

- What would it be like to give up your sense of control and truly believe that God knows what's best for you? Give an example of a specific situation in your life where this thinking could change your life.

  _____

  _____

- Can you give an example of a heart's desire you prayed about and then experienced its becoming a reality? How did that affect you?

  _____

  _____

4. Zechariah praised God for His timing.

Zechariah could never have imagined it would take years, or even decades, before God would answer his prayers. When we pray we get to know what God is concerned about and we get to know what He is like. But we also get a picture of His timing. When our prayer is answered with "No, My child, not today," then that is His will.

Even if we don't understand.

God wants us to keep seeking Him and to praise Him along the journey. No matter how long we wait to see the answer to our prayers.

Our praise needs to come before and after the answered prayer. God deserves our praise and honor regardless of our personal comfort and needs. Zechariah understood this. He went to Jerusalem to praise God and offer prayers on behalf of the people even though twenty years of his own personal prayer for a child had gone unanswered.

This is why God tells us in Scripture that Zechariah was faithful. We want to be people like that, too. In season and out, we should have an overwhelming and immediate response to the very real presence of God. Zechariah showed us what that should look like. Pure, heart-filled praise.

- Have you ever had an experience where God provided and the first thing that came from your mouth was "Praise the Lord!" Why? What happened to you in that instant that caused you to respond in that way?

_____

_____

- Now let's look at the reverse. Think of

a season in your life of confusion and waiting. Did you find yourself saying, "Praise God!"? Why or why not?

_____

_____

- Why is it important to be faithful in prayer and praise toward God regardless of your current situation? What happens to your focus when you live this way? Give an example.

_____

_____

Homework: Practice two things this week. First, practice praising God in all situations. When something goes wrong, you feel confused, or the answers are not coming, immediately find a reason to quietly thank God. Second, practice being silent. Make a decision to listen; talk as infrequently as possible for a period of time or for a few days. Do this individually at home. Come prepared to talk about both these experiences.

STUDY 3
JOHN THE BAPTIST
THE CHOSEN COUSIN

DAY 1
Read Luke 3:1–20

As a prophet, John willingly
took on his role of preparing
the way for Jesus.

I love that the Bible gives us a look at the
very best of John the Baptist. That's the case
in this passage. Luke references the prophet
Isaiah when he summarizes John's activity
on the planet as an influencer, a minister,
and a baptizer: "Prepare the way for the
Lord, make straight paths for him. Every
valley shall be filled in, every mountain and
hill made low. The crooked roads shall
become straight, the rough ways smooth."
(See Isaiah 40:3–4 NIV.)

John did not live long. I doubt his life

ended the way he expected it would. But still he is one of the most revered characters from the story of Jesus. One of the most passionate of Jesus's family members. For those who love God, it isn't the days in our life that define us. It's the life in our days. The obedience and passion to live for God and His purpose.

- John spent his life waiting for God's direction. Not until he heard from the Lord did his real life of being "awake" to God's calling begin. What do you think it means to be "awake" spiritually?

  _____

  _____

- John lived on a limited diet of locusts and honey. He dwelled away from people for much of his life. He was unpopular with the highest human authorities. His career was cut short because he was thrown into prison. He had his head cut off. Sometimes we covet the roles of people in authority. Do you wish you could trade places with him? Do you wish God gave you

John's role? Why or why not?

_____

_____

- God is calling you to do something. What is that? How does John the Baptist's obedience speak to you about what God is calling you to do?

_____

_____

John spoke the truth urgently with
boldness and clarity.

It's easy to read about John's time at the
Jordan River and cringe just a little. "Not
very politically correct," we might say. Or
"Not sure John was very loving." But understand this: There was an urgency to John's
calling. He told the truth the way we might
if we saw someone driving full bore toward
the edge of a cliff. "Stop! Turn around!
You're going to destroy yourself!"

John loved the people at the Jordan River
and people for all time when he preached
with such boldness and clarity. He cared
enough to call out the sin in their lives
and ours. He was a prophet, after all. The
voice of warning for a generation. For all
time.

This was what John came to do for Jesus.

- John spent his life reflecting on spiritual things. When taking time to think
  on spiritual matters, what do you

wonder about? What makes you curious?

_____

_____

- Do you know someone who seems to understand what God is doing and why? What is he or she like?

_____

_____

- When have you felt led to speak boldly about a spiritual matter? Discuss that time.

_____

_____

John took the long view even when he didn't understand what was happening.

A prophet is the one who sees a bigger picture. Like an eagle soaring above a field, the prophet is able to discern what most on the ground cannot. He is led by the Spirit and identifies patterns and senses things about the future. With great boldness, he speaks about what he sees. John the Baptist was tasked with the work of raking up hard ground: It had been four hundred years. The Israelites hadn't heard from God. They weren't close to ready to receive the Messiah and His message.

John dedicated his entire life to this difficult task of preparing the way for Jesus. He reminded the Israelites of their sins and pagan lifestyle. He made them aware of how they had fallen short. And when he was arrested, he stayed true to the task he had been born for. When the burden became too much to bear, John questioned. But he accepted the answer without doubting.

316

- In John's story we look in on him in his cell and consider what that must've been like. Have you ever felt as though your story was not turning out the way you had hoped? How did you respond? How did John respond?

_____

_____

- Jesus responded to John's desperate question by describing His miraculous actions. What proof of Jesus's being real have you seen in your life? Explain.

_____

_____

- Have you ever doubted God the way John did? Explain the situation. How did you handle it? What was the result?

_____

_____

John created a crisis of faith in whoever
would listen.

It's uncomfortable to wake up. Most people
prefer the comfort of denial.

John's desire was to help his fellow Jews
see that their captivity to sin was much
greater than that of being enslaved to
Romans. Before he gave them the good
news, he began with the bad.

Before you can experience the hero in any
story, you must have a critical situation. A
terrible need. I'm a storyteller. But I can't
tell a story without conflict. The story brings
satisfaction only when hope and redemption can be shown in the face of great
struggle.

That's what John did in Luke 3: He
showed people the contrast by exposing the
lies and fabrications of Jewish society. He
revealed the brokenness of a life lived apart
from God's divine plan. Only then would
the people be ready for the good news of a
Savior.

- John taught that the consequence of living in death is that you will not be included in God's plan. This was the summary of his teaching at the Jordan River. Can you think of a time when you were in denial about something and after experiencing crisis, you looked at life from a whole new perspective? Describe it.

  _____

  _____

- Why did John the Baptist say that one was coming whose purpose was greater than his? What do you think of John the Baptist's bold approach when he taught people at the Jordan River? Have you ever been bold in love about the message of Jesus?

  _____

  _____

John was unafraid of controversy. He understood that people had a crucial need for his message.

Prophets are like trainers who make you do one last pushup or get on the treadmill for a final two-minute run. You don't like them while they are inflicting pain. But when you can breathe easily on that weekend hike, they're the ones you text with words of thanks.

We all need someone to push us. Someone to help us see what we're lacking, what we need.

Someone to wake us up.

- Have you ever been frustrated with someone's approach to sharing God's love and truth? Is it possible that different approaches are appropriate for different people? Explain.

_____

_____

- When John confronted people with

320

their sins, they asked, "What should we do then?" John got people's attention. He was an effective communicator. God has equipped all people to share the truth and love of Jesus. How are you best equipped to do that? What is your strength in telling people the good news of the gospel? Give an example.

_____

_____

• How can you use your gifts to show love to others?

_____

_____

> **Read Psalm 139:13–16**

John the Baptist understood his calling, and that only he could finish that task.

1. John knew his purpose.

God has a specific design on your life. And you are not alone. So while we can learn much from John's commitment and intentional living, we would never want to be just like John. Your role and mine are different. So in a difficult situation, rather than ask, "What would John the Baptist [or anyone else] do?" the better question would be, "Jesus, what do You want me to do? In my unique design and story? How should I reflect Your will and way?"

My kids all have different talents, different callings and passions. I'm delighted when I see the athlete forgoing a movie to work out. And I'm equally grateful when the songwriter is up late at night at the piano creating music for God. I love their differences. The key for any of us is to identify that calling the way John the Baptist did.

- What role has God given you for this season in your life? What part of that role is difficult for you?

  _____

  _____

- Do you wish that role was different? Why or why not?

  _____

  _____

2. John understood that God's work required ambition.

John's approach was confident and aggressive. He preached with a boldness we talked about earlier. Some might have seen John at work at the Jordan River and rolled their eyes. They might have accused him of being overly zealous or ambitious. Some might have said he tried too hard, was too pushy.

But John seemed to understand that his was a job given by God alone. God had called John to warn the people, to prepare the way. And John did it with every bit of his energy, emotion, and effort. In the same way, when God calls us to do a job, we must put our entire being into the task. Heart, mind, body, and soul.

- Are you willing to work harder than ever before, or be bolder than ever before to accomplish God's calling on your life? What would that look like?

  _____

  _____

- How can you be fully committed — ambitious, even — for God, and yet still humble and loving? Explain.

  _____

  _____

- Most of us have a desert of sorts, a place or way of life we must accept before we can find the true calling of God on our lives. What is God asking you to give up or change in order to better do His will?

  _____

  _____

3. God's dream for us is bigger than the dreams we have for ourselves.

John the Baptist knew he was born to prepare the way for the Savior. But he never could have imagined that plan would include being murdered for the cause of the gospel. Still, John's death rallied the followers of Jesus. It gave Jesus an object lesson about the cost of following Him. In the long run, the story works out. Jesus even let John know before his death that heaven was better.

Some define "leadership" as "influence." Worldly leaders during John's day had wealth, prestige, titles, and earthly power. Yet they did nothing to redeem the world. They lived for a different agenda. Their names do not give us hope. We don't remember them.

Rather, history remembers John the Baptist and his calling, his preaching.

- What about your role in God's story is a struggle for you? Explain.

  _____

  _____

- Are you willing to accept and embrace your role as John did?

  _____

  _____

- Can you think of a difficult time in

your life? What good came from it?

_____

_____

Homework: If John the Baptist singled you out in a crowd, what would he say? Write down your thoughts and why. Share your answers with the group.

STUDY 4
ELIZABETH

THE FAITHFUL AUNT

DAY 1
Read Luke 1:5–25

Elizabeth learned that God is seldom
early but never late.

Elizabeth was older, "well along in years,"
and past the point of childbearing.

When I created a fictional story around
Elizabeth I thought about how old she
might be. First Timothy 5:9 says that no
woman should be put on the list of widows
unless she was over the age of sixty. Since
women had children very young in those
days, Elizabeth's friends would've borne
children in their late teens. By the time Elizabeth was in her mid- to late thirties, her
friends were having grandchildren.

Because of that, and because Scripture

doesn't say exactly how well along in years Elizabeth was, I chose that she'd be thirty-five or older. But Elizabeth was also able to celebrate the fact that God had answered her prayers at that time, rather than earlier. Otherwise John wouldn't have been the prophet sent to prepare the way for Jesus.

- Elizabeth was clearly sad that the deepest desire of her heart had not been met. Sometimes our pain helps us know where we most need God. What do you think that meant for Elizabeth? What does it mean for you?

  _____

  _____

- Describe a time when your prayers were not answered in your timing. What did God teach you through that process? Explain.

  _____

  _____

Elizabeth prepared the way for Mary in
birth — maybe also in death.

If Elizabeth was in her mid-thirties when
she gave birth to John, she would've been in
her mid-sixties when John reported to the
Jordan River. The Bible doesn't tell us
whether Elizabeth lived that long. But for
the sake of my storytelling I asked if it was
possible. Since it was, I chose to write about
it.

So we have a beautiful picture of Elizabeth living out her life as a mentor. Clearly
she prepared the way for Mary in birth. The
Bible says when Elizabeth was in her sixth
month, Mary came rushing to her with
news about her own pregnancy. How long
did Mary stay?

Three months.

Though the Bible doesn't tell us whether
Mary stayed long enough to see John born,
it's certainly likely. Elizabeth's role was to
bring comfort and assurance to the mother
of Jesus. Possibly even to show Mary what
birth looked like.

So it is possible that Elizabeth was also there to show Mary what death looked like. After John was murdered, Mary may have visited her dear cousin. Either way, Elizabeth accepted her role as preparing the way for Mary.

When Elizabeth saw Mary she immediately declared, "Blessed are you among women, and blessed is the child you will bear!" Elizabeth was also helping her young cousin realize, *Mary, you didn't deserve this. This isn't something you did on your own. Another strengthens you. You have been given a gift. You are empowered by the Almighty.*

One more thing. Elizabeth assured Mary that the child Mary was carrying was the Messiah. How? By telling her that her own baby, John, leapt in her womb the moment Mary appeared. Elizabeth's son became in that moment the first to worship Jesus — a detail Elizabeth felt compelled to share. Part of her way of preparing Mary.

Elizabeth gives us so many beautiful examples of mentoring in this very short exchange.

- Elizabeth's role was to help Mary better understand her role. Few special songs or stories have been written about Elizabeth. Have you ever been in the presence of someone with more fame, more Twitter followers, more Facebook friends? How did that make you feel?

_____

_____

- When have you been asked to lead the way for someone else? Explain the situation.

_____

_____

- Elizabeth was a mentor and an encourager. Whom have you had the privilege of mentoring and encouraging? Did that situation make you feel closer to God? Explain.

_____

_____

Elizabeth accepted her role
in God's story.

It's worth noting what did not happen when Elizabeth and Mary met in those early days. She could have thought about the pain she was dealing with as an older woman going through pregnancy. She could've felt she deserved to carry the Messiah. After all, she had waited longer.

It would've been easy for Elizabeth to start comparing herself to Mary. Jealousy could've taken root.

Instead, Elizabeth is a wonderful example to mothers. She chose not to compare or envy but to rejoice in the blessing of another. When we bless someone else and focus not on what we lack but on what we have, we become thankful.

Elizabeth was full of gratitude, joy, and praise. When these characteristics describe your life, you'll find it hard to complain. Elizabeth was a woman who lived under scrutiny and with rejection. A woman with longings unfulfilled. She entered and most likely finished her life helping Mary care for the Messiah who would save her, and giving birth to a son who would give his life for that same Savior.

Favored? Yes.

Her attitude: thankful.

- Have you ever struggled with envy because of someone else's success?

  _____

  _____

- Filled with the Holy Spirit, Elizabeth immediately rejoiced with Mary about her blessing. Sometimes that is not our first response when hearing someone else's good news. Can you remember a time when your earliest reaction was not positive? Share an example.

  _____

  _____

Elizabeth's suffering brought perspective.

Elizabeth lived many years without a child. She knew what it was like to go without. So when she finally had the chance to have a baby, Elizabeth was overcome with gratitude and wonder. She even spent the first several months of her pregnancy in seclusion — probably savoring every little change in her body. When we really feel our pain and let God heal us, we are blessed with a deeper appreciation for the things of life. Only God can touch us in that deep place and allow us to see His threads of redemption.

When our youngest son, Austin, was born with a congenital heart defect, we were faced with the very real possibility that he wouldn't live beyond his first few weeks. He was rushed into emergency surgery with less than a 50 percent chance of surviving. During that season of suffering, even after God healed Austin in surgery, Donald and I gained great perspective on the purpose of life. The preciousness of it. Because of Austin, we never take a day for granted.

Elizabeth was probably much the same way.

- Elizabeth's culture considered child-lessness a curse from God. Have you ever been hurt in a deep place, and like Elizabeth, felt shunned or rejected? How did you respond? Has God healed you of that pain?

  _____

  _____

- How did God redeem Elizabeth's story?

  _____

  _____

- How can suffering sometimes be a gift? Explain.

  _____

  _____

Celebrating others reminds us to
hold on to joy.

The best way to stay happy when everyone
around you seems more blessed? Celebrate
with them! Really. And this is exactly what
Elizabeth did when she said, "But why am I
so favored, that the mother of my Lord
should come to me?"

When we celebrate the blessings of others
— genuinely, with our whole hearts — we
do something God always calls us to do: We
take our eyes off ourselves and serve others.
In doing so, we ward off jealousy. Not only
does rejoicing with them allow us to participate in their blessing, it forces us to evalu-
ate what we are thankful for.

And celebrate.

- Why is it hard sometimes to celebrate
  the goodness in other people's lives?

  _____

  _____

- Think of a time when you were able to

truly celebrate someone else's good news. What was that like?

_____

_____

- How does rejoicing in someone else's blessing allow us to participate in it?

_____

_____

Read Psalm 100

Elizabeth set an example for Mary and showed us what a mentor looks like.

1. Elizabeth accepted her role with gratitude.

A college professor tried an exercise with his students: he challenged them to go twenty-four hours without complaining. They were to keep a journal or piece of paper with them and write down every time they began to complain. Eventually he did this same exercise with adults. Over the years only a handful could honestly say they didn't complain.

There was more to the experiment. Students were also asked to write down what they were thankful for in three categories: Things, People, and Others. For the next twenty-four hours they were to read the list four times: First thing in the morning. After lunch. After dinner. Before bed.

This professor said every time he does this

338

exercise, the class changes from that day forward. Students are happier, more conversational. More attentive to others. Elizabeth could have complained about her late pregnancy or felt jealous over Mary being blessed with giving birth to the Savior. Instead she lived in gratitude.

- What do you think about a challenge to go twenty-four hours without complaining? Do you think you could do it?

  _____

  _____

- Write a list of what you are thankful for. How do you feel when you see those things written down?

  _____

  _____

- If you choose to do this same exercise with your group, be sure to read over your gratitude list four times a day: First thing in the morning. After lunch. After dinner. Before bed. Now can you relate a little more to Elizabeth?

  _____

  _____

2. Like Elizabeth, when we celebrate we are compelled to worship.

Elizabeth understood something many of us go a lifetime trying to grasp: it is hard to praise God when we feel jealous.

If, however, we review what is good in our lives, if we spend our day being thankful and happy for others, our perspective changes. Our hearts change, too.

Elizabeth celebrated Mary's good news, and as she did her unborn baby leapt in her womb. She was the first to understand the connection between celebration and worship.

Before you even get around to praising God for how wonderful He is, lead with, "I am so thankful!" Be sure to be thankful for the good things in the lives of others, too.

Gratitude just might change your life. The way it did for Elizabeth.

- How will you display gratitude today for the blessings of someone else? Could you write someone a note or email and share how happy you are for his or her success?

_____

_____

- How will you remember to thank God today for your own blessings?

_____

_____

- Remember, we are not of this world. We are children of God, living in His kingdom even here on earth. There is much to celebrate. What can you change about your life so that people will remember you as one who celebrated God's goodness in all situations?

_____

_____

Homework: Find a psalm that best describes your thankfulness and share it with the group. How do you relate to the psalmist's declarations?

STUDY 5
JAMES

THE DOUBTING BROTHER

DAY 1
Read Mark 6:1–3

Trust what Jesus says about Himself.

Imagine you're James and you are living in the household of Joseph of Nazareth. Imagine working for the family construction company. Picture having a brother who did everything right. At home He never forgets to say please and thank you. He brushes and flosses His teeth every day and no one has to remind Him.

You and your sibling go to a construction project and He catches on faster than anyone. He is better than Home Depot with nails. He is a better designer than Martha Stewart. Come to find out Frank Lloyd Wright got all his ideas from Him. He is just that good. At times people even label Him a perfectionist. And He is your brother.

Talk about trying to measure up.

So it follows that when the perfect child left the family business to go into ministry, James had questions. For instance, what made Jesus qualified to be a religious teacher? He was the construction guy, and He was in line to inherit his father's business. Why would Jesus abandon the family?

Jesus left home. Time passed and when He returned, He brought with Him a bunch of rowdy fellows He called His "disciples." People were confused. Wasn't He just the carpenter's son? James had to feel so much confusion. Jesus Himself had to feel the pain of being misunderstood — especially by his next youngest brother, James.

- James grew up with Jesus. Can you imagine having Jesus as your brother? What do you think it would be like?

  _____

  _____

- Do you think James ever compared himself to Jesus? Do you think others in town — the local rabbi, perhaps —

compared James to his brother? What would that have felt like?

_____

_____

Stand up for those being wronged.

There was Jesus in His hometown and the people in His community were about to murder Him, throw Him from the cliff. Most theologians agree that James would've been part of that crowd — or certainly understanding of their actions.

Notice what *isn't* in the passage. There is no mention that the crowd took Jesus to the edge of the cliff and James said, "Hey, don't touch my brother."

Nowhere does it say that James shouted, "Hey! If you're throwing Him off, you're throwing me off."

James had opportunities to stand up for his oldest brother, Jesus. But instead he either stayed silent or joined the accusing, doubting crowd.

- James had a comfortable view of Jesus as his brother: Jesus the carpenter. When Jesus claimed to be God, James shrank back. Have you ever struggled with being bold for Jesus? Explain the situation. How did you feel later?

_____

_____

- Do you ever feel the temptation to try to please everyone in the room? If so, does that ever feel exhausting?

_____

_____

- James tried to please his mother and brothers by being intently focused on Jesus's return to the family. How was his focus off?

_____

_____

Believe the best about others.

One thing is certain about James: he and Jesus's other brothers thought Jesus was crazy because of His claim to be the Messiah. They didn't believe the best about Him. Not even close.

The Bible gives us all we need to picture it. Jesus and the religious establishment had a major confrontation. James and the rest of the family didn't like Jesus making waves, so they attempted to "take charge of him." Yes, James wanted to control the person responsible for creating the planet.

Now, to be fair, James really thought he and the others were doing the right thing. They thought they were protecting Jesus and their family's reputation. But Jesus was unaffected. He didn't start pacing the room, wringing His hands, second-guessing Himself.

Instead, Jesus confidently declared that He was serving exactly the way God had called Him to serve. Jesus explained that His mother and brothers were those who heard His words and obeyed them. Then He calmly continued teaching.

Hardly the picture of someone out of his mind.

- James and his family thought Jesus was going crazy. How do you feel when those closest to you think you are unstable?

  _____

  _____

- What do you think motivated James to treat Jesus this way?

  _____

  _____

- Have you ever been embarrassed by a family member? How did you handle that situation? How do you feel about it now?

  _____

  _____

Don't mock what you don't understand.

Imagine how James must have felt, having been publicly shunned by Jesus. James thought *family* meant the people sitting around the dinner table. The ones running the family business. But Jesus had been very clear back at the house down the street.

Family was better defined as those who shared faith in Him.

James must have been angry and hurt. We see in these verses a sense of sarcasm and mockery. *Sure, Jesus,* James might as well have said. *Go on and do Your miracles. Don't stay here and do them in secret. Let all the world know.*

Bitterness. Words that come from a wounded heart. This was James.

But it was not the end of his story.

It doesn't have to be the end of yours.

- Has someone ever publicly corrected or rebuked you? How did that feel? How did it change your relationship with that person?

_____

_____

- We have two choices when someone hurts us: We can talk with that person and find a resolution. Or we can let bitterness take root. James chose the latter. How can bitterness harm us? Give an example.

_____

_____

- How have you seen sarcasm harm a relationship? Explain.

_____

_____

James's visit from the resurrected Jesus
changed his life.

If James tried to stop the crucifixion of Christ, it certainly is not documented. Again in my storytelling I used this as a signpost. Was it possible James was standing in the distant shadows, watching Jesus be put to death? I think so. If he did, imagine his heartache when Jesus died, when the earth shook.

When it became painfully obvious that after all this time, Jesus had been telling the truth.

He was God in the flesh. The Messiah.

However devastated James must've felt, we know this much from the Bible. In 1 Corinthians 15:7, we read that Jesus made an appearance to James. One-on-one.

And after that James became a disciple. He would spend the rest of his days serving Christ, telling the Jewish people about Jesus and His plan for salvation. In the book of Acts, James emerges as a prominent leader. He becomes the pastor of the first church organized and established in Jerusalem.

In fact, the book of James was written by James, the brother of Jesus. My fictionalization of James and this Bible study will hopefully lead you to read that book with a new perspective. Especially the part in James 1:27 where James says that perfect religion is to take care of orphans and widows.

Caring for orphans: the people who are not blood-related to us.

James, the one who once believed family was defined by the dinner table at home started his letter adamant about an entirely different view. Family are those who believe Jesus is God.

Talk about perfect redemption.

- Jesus came back and met with James individually. What do you think that moment was like?

  _____

  _____

- How did you feel when you first recognized your sin, and that Jesus died on a cross to pay the price for it? Describe your salvation experience.

_____

_____

- If you haven't acknowledged that Jesus is God, what is holding you back? Talk to a Christian friend or family member about this. Commit to ask God to show Himself to you — the way Jesus showed Himself to James.

_____

_____

Read James 1

In his later days, James understood the power of prayer.

1. Prayer and listening to God are efforts of the will.

James experienced a dramatic change from his days as an unbeliever to his time as a servant of Christ. Clearly, he spent time seeking God and listening to Him.

What about us? After we enter a quiet place to be with the Lord, sometimes the most difficult thing to do is pray. We are distracted, unfocused, and often unable to find the words we want to speak.

Here's the thing, friend. Prayer takes practice.

Imagine you are talking to your closest buddy. The one who knows everything about you and loves you anyway. Don't give up. It gets easier.

If you will swing the door of your life fully open and, as Matthew 6:6 says, pray to your Father, who is in the secret place, everything

355

in your life will be marked with the lasting imprint of the presence of God.

- Why do you think James spent so much time in prayer? Could there be a connection between James's prayer time and how much he may have missed Jesus as the brother who sat across from him when they were kids?

_____

_____

- Prayer makes us closer to God. If you practice it, you will never go back. Talk about your prayer experience. Does prayer come easily for you? Why or why not?

_____

_____

2. Prayer produces patience.

James could have given in to despair during the time Jesus was in the tomb. He could've killed himself, the way Judas did. Instead he was there waiting when Jesus found him three days later. The reason is probably something we learn later about James — that he loved to pray.

Prayer is a posture, really, that shows our

desire to go to God and worship Him, thank Him, and then present our requests according to His will. But sometimes we measure our satisfaction in prayer only by what we get out of it. Whether or not we say it out loud, we often think, *I prayed for ten minutes today, and Jesus hasn't answered my prayer. What's the point?*

Living in a hurried society, we have trouble waiting. In our worst moments, we might even think we're better off to handle a situation ourselves than to spend time praying about it.

But prayer is not a hurried thing. It's a conversation. It's often been said that we don't have time *not* to pray. Maybe the change you're looking for could begin with that very thought.

The way it maybe did for James in the days after the crucifixion.

- James became a patient teacher of the ways of Jesus. What does that say about him?

  _____

  _____

- Are your prayers marked by patience? Give an example.

_____

_____

- Can you remember a time when your prayers felt like true conversation with Jesus? Talk about that time.

_____

_____

3. Prayer includes us in God's story of redemption.

James understood that when we pray, we become a part of God's story. In James 1:5, James seems to say that if we want wisdom, we have to hang out with God. The way James once hung out with Jesus around the house.

In the time spent together we begin to value what He values. When we get into relational rhythm with God, the prayers that flow from us, flow from the heart of God. Those prayers are naturally answered because we are just closing the loop.

This is an important thing to understand regarding our desires and what we feel we need. In prayer we begin to discern where those desires find their origin, the Spirit or the flesh. If our desires are His desires anyway, then prayer just gives us a chance to be involved in the way He is engaging the world and moving the story forward.

Prayer gives you the blessing of being included in God's story!

Heaven is not just future. It is present. The eternal is accessible here and now.

James expressed a valuable lesson, one he must've learned from spending time with Jesus: faith without works is dead. If we really have faith — and James knew about this because he lived so long without it — we want to know God more.

Why do you think Satan puts massive effort into creating distractions that keep you and me from time in prayer? The answer is simple: the villain in this story wants to keep us from knowing God.

Another wonderful reason to pray more.

- Do you ever get frustrated with God regarding how He does or doesn't respond to your prayers? Read James 5:16. What do you think this means?

  _____

  _____

- Is it easy for you to find time to pray?

Why or why not?

_____

_____

- What might your life be like if you knew God better? Do you know some-one who seems to know the Lord more closely than you? What is his or her life like?

_____

_____

Homework: Like James, will you take the time to talk to God and really listen to Him this week? Make an appointment with God each day. Select a location and decide on a specific amount of time. Discuss what your experience is like when you gather again.

STUDY 6
MARY

THE LOVING MOTHER

DAY 1
Read Luke 1:26–38

Mary was willing to obey God, whatever
the assignment.

The story of Mary touches many of us
deeply.

Just imagine for a moment what it must
have been like for Mary, going to sleep the
night of the angel's visit, and waking the
next morning, asking, *Was yesterday a
dream? Did that really happen? Did I really
visit with an angel who told me that somehow
I would become pregnant?*

How mind-blowing! What we discover in
Luke 1 is that Mary realized the significance
of that moment because she sat down and
wrote a worship song. She was full of joy-

ous anticipation.

- How would you respond if an angel showed up and spoke to you while you were sitting on the front porch? How do you think Mary felt when the angel visited her?

  _____

  _____

- There were many costs to being the mother of Jesus. In those early days, what must some of the costs have been? What are the challenges to following God in your life?

  _____

  _____

- Luke 2:19 says, "But Mary treasured up all these things and pondered them in her heart." What is the connection between pondering the goodness of a situation and handling the costs involved? How often do you reflect on your life and consider your blessings?

  _____

  _____

Mary was full of faith.

With an angel of the Lord standing before her, announcing that she would be pregnant with God's son, Mary had just one innocent question: How was it possible, since she was a virgin? She asked it and accepted the answer without reservation. Her words stay with us to this day: "I am the Lord's servant."

We often ask God about His will. "God, what do You want for my life? What's my vocation, my career?" "Whom should I marry?" "Should we have children?" "Should we buy a house?"

As we ask these questions, we call out to God for direction, and often His response comes to us as a whisper. We wish it came on the wings of an angel, but usually we patiently (or impatiently) wait and He reveals His will over time. Once Mary understood what God called her to do, she embraced God's plan for her life.

What a beautiful example of faith.

- Have you ever met someone like Mary, who had a quiet confidence, unwavering conviction, and unshakable faith in God? Give an example. What do you admire about him or her?

_____

_____

- In the story we go with Mary on a journey of blessing and hardship, celebration and brokenness. Tell of a time when you experienced pain and struggle. Did your faith help you through that time, the way it helped Mary? Why or why not?

_____

_____

Mary praised God even in uncertainty.

Mary was the first of the family of Jesus to respond to unbelievable uncertainty with one beautiful response: praise.

She began a praise song that starts with the words, "My soul glorifies the Lord and my spirit rejoices in God my Savior."

Mary was about to be shunned and rejected by her townspeople. She would risk rejection by Joseph, the one she loved. Yet she responded to the angel's news by expressing how her spirit rejoiced in God's plan for her life.

Christian singer Jeremy Camp is one of my friends. I wrote a foreword for his book *Walk by Faith,* and in that book Jeremy talks about losing his first wife to cancer. The moment she died, he dropped to his knees and praised God.

That's the sort of response we see in Mary. A response that turns logic upside down and reveals trust in God.

- Mary did not argue with God about

whether He made the right decision in choosing her to carry His Son. She simply accepted His grace and praised God. What else about Mary's praise song stands out to you? What can you learn from it?

_____

_____

- Are you tempted to accept only a portion of God's goodness and not all of what He offers? Why or why not?

_____

_____

- Read Psalm 139:1–12. What do you think this worship song is about? Mary would've known this Scripture and had nine months to ponder it while the Savior was being formed in her womb. What are your thoughts on the sanctity of life?

_____

_____

Mary was a peaceful woman.

Mary's life was in complete chaos. But the Savior of the world was cradled in her arms. What did Mary do? Did she cry or doubt or fall into a crippling depression? No. Mary treasured these things in her heart.

She had peace in the midst of the storm.

Never mind the smell and sounds of animals in the dark, dank stable. Mary was at peace enough that she didn't miss the moment. Her Messiah, her rescuer, lay sleeping in her embrace.

What about us? Life is busy. We are inundated with work and chores, kids and bills; the everydayness of life can steal our time and our joy. But even in the midst of the chaos, there is something to treasure. A reason for peace.

The sound of your child's voice — he or she won't sound the same when they are older.

The hand-drawn picture on the counter, the echo of laughter as someone shares a funny story. The beautiful sky outside your window, the hug of someone you love. The moments are there if we would only pay attention.

See, today won't last. No matter how busy or mundane it feels, today is a gift. It comes but once. We keep it only one way. By doing what Mary did. Having peace in the storm, and treasuring the priceless moments in our hearts.

- Mary knew who she was because she belonged to God and was chosen by Him. She considered herself God's servant. How could that have brought Mary peace? How could having that attitude bring you peace in your situation? Explain.

  _____

  _____

- What moments from the past week should you treasure in your heart? Did you? Explain the situation and how you feel about it now.

  _____

  _____

Mary received grace and help to survive
the greatest loss a mother can face.

Imagine being Mary, knowing that an angry mob was about to kill your innocent son.

If not for the strength and grace of God, Mary could not have stood at the foot of the cross. She had spent her life protecting the Messiah. She was one of His followers from the beginning. But in the final moments before His death, she was close to the cross.

How could she bear it?

Because her trust in God from the beginning gave her grace for the moment. And because she trusted Jesus to take care of her, whatever she might need. As it turned out, Mary did have needs. We know this because in this passage Jesus declared that John was to take care of Mary. And that Mary would indeed have a son in John.

You see the connection?

Mary trusted God from the beginning. And now in the most desperate hour, when the angel's voice must've felt very far away,

Jesus helped Mary hold on to her sanity. He gave her a way to stand up under the pain of losing Him.

This is the promise from God, friend. We will go through dark times. John 16:33 says that in this world we "will have trouble." But we can be all right with that, because Jesus has overcome the world.

Mary at the foot of the cross of Jesus is a picture of that.

- Describe a very sad or dark time in your life. How did you survive it?

  _____

  _____

- What does that situation say about the faithfulness of God?

  _____

  _____

- How has God provided for you in times of need?

  _____

  _____

Read Job 38:1–18

Mary trusted God no matter the circumstances.

1. Mary was willing to live life without control.

It's easy to think we have control in our lives. "It's under control," we sometimes say. "Everything's in control now." Or, "Sure hope we don't lose control of the situation!"

But the truth is — we can't lose control. We can never lose something we never had to begin with.

Did you control your conception? Did you breathe life into yourself? Do you have a say in the number of days you'll experience? The number of pages in your story?

Of course not.

Friend, when we say we are giving our lives to God, we are actually giving them *back* to God. We are already His. After all, our spirits are His creation. The body, the container, is only a temporary residence,

371

and soon it will return to dust. We often fail to see life from an accurate perspective.

We are not in control.

And because of that our tendency sometimes is to run from God, thinking we are better off trying to control our own lives than offering them for His service. But in our fierce determination to find control, we lose faith.

Faith is the opposite of control. Hebrews 11:1 says, "Faith is being sure of what we hope for and certain of what we do not see." In other words, we do not have control. But in faith we can have hope and certainty.

That's the life Mary lived.

It can be our lives, too.

- How strong is your desire for control in your life? Give an example.

  _____

  _____

- How is faith the opposite of control? Describe a time when you had to rely on faith.

  _____

  _____

- Jesus was faithful to carry Mary

through the uncertainty of His death on a cross. How does this speak to you?

_____

_____

2. Mary understood her value was in God.

Mary never would've wanted people celebrating her except for one reason: She was chosen by God. She was His servant. That was the reason people would call her "blessed" for all time.

Mary understood this.

In Mary's prayer in Luke 1, she did not claim goodness of her own but said she would be remembered among women because of God's initiative. Because of what God had done.

What about us? Where does our worth come from? Does it come from God, and the fact that He created us for His purpose? For His good plans? Or does it come from some false sense of control and worldly identity?

I've written a number of novels that show people finding their worth in celebrity and fame. Some find it in youth or fitness or beauty.

Not Mary.

She knew she was blessed because God had chosen her. Not because of anything she had done or any connection she had to the right people. Always, only God defined Mary.

Maybe it's time to see ourselves through Mary's eyes.

- What defines your worth? Explain.

  _____

  _____

- Tell of a time when you were tempted to see yourself through the eyes of the world. How did that affect you? Explain.

  _____

  _____

- How does it make you feel to know you are the child of the King? How can you better live in this reality?

  _____

  _____

3. Mary's life was characterized by constant communication with God.

Mary was a woman of prayer from the very beginning.

The first mention of Mary in the Bible includes reflection and prayer. She began praying for her son, the Savior who would come from God. The last mention of Mary (Acts 1:14) includes reflection and prayer. It is interesting that the family members closest to Jesus — Mary, James, John the Baptist — had such deep and passionate prayer lives.

See, friend, this is why we're taking a closer look at the family of Jesus. The costs they faced and characteristics of these special people.

So much to learn from them.

Especially Mary.

- Mary understood that if she was to be a woman of obedience and peace, she needed to pray. What is the connection between peace and prayer?

  _____

  _____

- Talk about a time when prayer changed

things in your life.

_____

_____

- What have you learned from the family of Jesus? Which character did you relate to most of all?

_____

_____

Homework: Start a prayer journal. You don't need to write in it every day. But keep track of the things you are praying about, the needs you are praying for. As you increase your consistency and faithfulness in prayer, go back to the journal and record God's answers. This will help you hold on to peace. It will help you stay close to the Creator. And it will help you remember the family of Jesus.

ACKNOWLEDGMENTS

A special thanks to Pastor Jamie George, who leads our Journey Church every Sunday. I asked Jamie to help me develop the teaching section at the end of this Bible study, and he was quick to say yes. You see, Jamie is a master storyteller, a man gifted to bring Scriptures to life week after week after week. I usually tell a different sort of story. So having Jamie's watchful eye poring over my short stories as I finished writing them gave me confidence that I had written only what was possible given the boundaries of the Bible. Jamie, thank you for inspiring me and our entire church to live in the story of Jesus and to remember this one important detail: the story is still being written everywhere someone believes in our Lord. And we are very much a part of it.

Also, thanks to my friends at Howard Books and Simon & Schuster, along with the talented team at LifeWay. This study wouldn't have happened without your fervent belief in me. Thank you for letting my passion for this project spill over onto all of you. I couldn't ask for a better team.

And to Rick Christian, my agent and friend — thank you for praying for me and my family, and for looking out for His plans for my life before thinking about anything the world might want. You are one in a million, Rick.

Thanks also to my mother, Anne Kingsbury, for loving my reader friends so well, and to Tricia, Kelsey, Kyle, and Sue for being an irreplaceable part of Life-Changing Fiction®. What a dream to work with all of you and to watch God use the power of story to change lives.

ABOUT THE AUTHOR

#1 *New York Times* bestselling novelist **Karen Kingsbury** is America's favorite inspirational storyteller, with more than 20 million copies of her award-winning books in print. Her last dozen books have topped bestseller charts and many of her novels are under development as major motion pictures. Karen lives in Tennessee with her husband Don and their five sons, three of whom are adopted from Haiti. Their actress daughter Kelsey is married to Christian recording artist Kyle Kupecky.